Patios and Walkways 1-2-3

Meredith BOOKS

Home Depot® Books
An imprint of Meredith® Books

Patios and Walkways 1-2-3®
Senior Editor: John P. Holms
Art Director: Tom Wegner
Writer: Jeff Day
Graphic Designer: Tim Abramowitz
Copy Chief: Terri Fredrickson
Copy and Production Editor: Victoria Forlini
Editorial Operations Manager: Karen Schirm
Managers, Book Production: Pam Kvitne,
Marjorie J. Schenkelberg, Rick von Holdt
Manufacturing and Inventory Control Manger: Mark Weaver
Contributing Copy Editor: Margaret Smith
Contributing Proofreaders: Heidi Johnson, Julie Cahalan,
      David Krause, Janet Anderson
Illustrators: Jim Swanson and Gwyn Raker
Indexer: Donald Glassman
Edit and Design Production Coordinator: Mary Lee Gavin
Editorial and Design Assistants: Renee E. McAtee,
      Karen McFadden

Meredith® Books
Editor in Chief: Linda Raglan Cunningham
Design Director: Matt Strelecki
Executive Editor, Gardening and Home Improvement:
      Benjamin W. Allen

Publisher: James D. Blume
Executive Director, Marketing: Jeffrey Myers
Executive Director, New Business Development: Todd M. Davis
Director, Sales-Home Depot: Robb Morris
Executive Director, Sales: Ken Zagor
Director, Operations: George A. Susral
Director, Production: Douglas M. Johnston
Business Director: Jim Leonard

Vice President and General Manager: Douglas J. Guendel

Meredith Publishing Group
President, Publishing Group: Stephen M. Lacy
Vice President-Publishing Director: Bob Mate

Meredith Corporation
Chairman and Chief Executive Officer: William T. Kerr
In Memoriam: E. T. Meredith III (1933-2003)

Photographers
Image Studios
Account Executive: Lisa Egan
Primary Photographers: Bill Rein, Glen Hartjes, Dave Wallace
Contributing Photographers: Dave Classon, Bill Kapinski,
      Shane Van Boxtel, John von Dorn
Construction Consultant: Rick Nadke
Assistants: Mike Clines, Roger Wilmers
Primary Stylist: BJ Hill
Contributing Stylists: Karla Kaphaem, Dawn Koehler

The Home Depot®
Licensing Specialist: Ilana Wilensky

Note to the Reader: Due to differing conditions, tools, and
individual skills, Meredith Corporation and The Home Depot®
assume no responsibility for any damages, injuries suffered, or
losses incurred as a result of following the information
published in this book. Before beginning any project, review
the instructions carefully, and if any doubts or questions
remain, consult local experts or authorities. Because codes and
regulations vary greatly, you always should check with
authorities to ensure that your project complies with all
applicable local codes and regulations. Always read and observe
all of the safety precautions provided by any tool
or equipment manufacturer, and follow all accepted
safety procedures.

The editors of Patios and Walkways 1-2-3® are dedicated to
providing accurate and helpful do-it-yourself information. We
welcome your comments about improving this book and ideas
for other books we might offer to home improvement
enthusiasts.

If you would like to purchase any of our home improvement,
cooking, crafts, gardening, or home decorating and design
books, check wherever quality books are sold. Or visit us at:
meredithbooks.com

Contact us by any of these methods:
Leave a voice message at: 800/678-2093
Write to: Meredith Books, Home Depot Books
      1716 Locust St.
      Des Moines, IA 50309–3023
Send e-mail to: hi123@mdp.com

Take our quick survey and enter to win a $1,000 gift card from The Home Depot®

WIN THIS CARD!
OFFICIAL SWEEPSTAKES RULES AND ENTRY DETAILS ON BACK.
No purchase necessary to enter or win.

Thank you for choosing this book! To serve you better, we'd like to know a little more about your interests. Please take a minute to fill out this survey and drop it in the mail. As an extra-special "thank-you" for your help, we'll enter your name into a drawing to win a $1,000 Home Depot Gift Card!

PLEASE MARK ONE CIRCLE PER LINE IN EACH OF THE NUMBERED COLUMNS BELOW WITH DARK PEN OR PENCIL:

1 My interest in the areas below is:

Cooking	High Interest	Average Interest	No Interest
Gourmet & Fine Foods	○	○	○
Quick & Easy	○	○	○
Healthy/Natural	○	○	○

Decorating	High Interest	Average Interest	No Interest
Country	○	○	○
Traditional	○	○	○
Contemporary	○	○	○

Do-It-Yourself	High Interest	Average Interest	No Interest
Home Repair	○	○	○
Remodeling	○	○	○
Home Decor (painting, wallpapering, window treatments, etc.)	○	○	○

Gardening	High Interest	Average Interest	No Interest
Flowers	○	○	○
Vegetables	○	○	○
Landscaping	○	○	○

2 My plans to do a project in the following areas within the next 6 months are:

	High Interest	Average Interest	No Interest
Bathroom Remodel	○	○	○
Kitchen Remodel	○	○	○
Storage Project	○	○	○
Plumbing	○	○	○
Wiring	○	○	○
Interior Painting	○	○	○
Window Treatments	○	○	○
Plant/Plan a Flower Garden	○	○	○
Plant/Plan a Vegetable Garden	○	○	○
Deck Building	○	○	○
Patio Building	○	○	○
Landscape Improvements	○	○	○

3 I estimate that I have spent this amount of money on home improvement projects in the past 6 months:
Less than $1,000 ○ $1,000-$2,500 ○ $2,500-$5,000 ○ $5,000-$10,000 ○ $10,000 or more ○

4 I purchased this book ○   This book was a gift ○

5 You *must* fill out all of the requested information below to enter to win a $1,000 Home Depot Gift Card.

Name:

Address: _____ Apt. or Suite # _____

Daytime telephone number: (   )

City:

State/Province: _____ Country: _____ Zip: _____

For D-I-Y trend research, please tell us your gender: Male ○   Female ○

Also, E-mail me with information of interest to me.

E-mail address:

Thank you for completing our survey! Please mail today to have your name entered to win a $1,000 Home Depot Gift Card. But hurry—one winner will be selected soon. See rules on back for entry deadline. To find more home improvement tips, visit www.homedepot.com or www.meredithbooks.com.

PW1004

Canadian customers:
See mailing details on back!

⬅

NO POSTAGE
NECESSARY
IF MAILED
IN THE
UNITED STATES

BUSINESS REPLY MAIL
FIRST-CLASS MAIL   PERMIT NO. 8359   DES MOINES, IA

POSTAGE WILL BE PAID BY ADDRESSEE

MEREDITH CORPORATION
HOME DEPOT 1-2-3 BOOKS (LN-104)
1716 LOCUST STREET
DES MOINES IA   50309-9708

▲ FOLD CAREFULLY ALONG ORANGE DASHED LINES ABOVE ▲

Take our quick survey and enter to win a $1,000 gift card from The Home Depot®

Expert Advice From The Home Depot ®

Patios and Walkways 1-2-3 ®

eredith ®

BOOKS

PATIOS AND WALKWAYS 1-2-3.

TABLE OF CONTENTS

SECTION 2: WALKWAYS

SECTION 3: PATIOS

SECTION 4: REPAIR AND MAINTENANCE

How to use this book

Abeautiful patio or walkway starts with good bones—secure foundations, level surfaces, tight stonework, and adequate drainage. These important elements provide functionality and can be attractive additions to the overall patio or walkway design.

Creating a beautiful patio or walkway involves basic construction techniques; working with materials such as stone, lumber, and concrete; and using many kinds of tools, from masonry saws to a hammer and tape measure. Successful installations mean:

- mastering some unfamiliar skills
- using the right tools and materials
- working safely
- doing the job right the first time

Patios and Walkways 1-2-3 can help. It's accessible, easy to use, and full of the right information. Here's how to get the most value out of *Patios and Walkways 1-2-3:*

TRUST THE WISDOM OF THE AISLES

A genuine desire to help people say, "I can do that!" is what the associates at The Home Depot® are all about. Landscaping experts from around the country have contributed their years of on-the-job experience and wisdom of the aisles to *Patios and Walkways 1-2-3*. They've created a hardworking, accurate, and easy-to-follow guide to the basics of patio and walkway construction.

THE ORGANIZING PRINCIPLE

Patios and Walkways 1-2-3 consists of four sections and 13 chapters that provide detailed coverage of the most common styles and techniques plus a comprehensive glossary, an index, and a resource guide.

TAKE A LOOK INSIDE!
Section One: Outdoor Design and Planning
This section covers the basics of design, choosing and working with materials, layout, excavation, and brick and paver patterns.

Section Two: Walkways
This section covers soft-set walkways, rustic paths, hard-bed paths, and boardwalks.

Section Three: Patios
This section covers soft-set patios, hard-bed patios, and steps and ramps.

Section Four: Repair and Maintenance
This section covers how to keep your patio or walkway in good repair.

DOING THE JOB—STEP-BY-STEP
All the projects include **complete instructions** along with detailed, **step-by-step photography** to ensure successful completion. You have everything you need to do the job right the first time following standards set by manufacturers and the trades—just like the pros.

TIPS, TRICKS, AND TIMESAVERS
Each page includes more than just how to do the job. To help you plan your project and to schedule your time, we've asked the experts to tell us how hard a job is, how long it takes them, and how long it might take you.

Skill Scales fill you in on the skills you'll need, time involved, and variables that might complicate the job.

Stuff You'll Need at the beginning of each project provides a materials list along with commonly needed tools. Additional features are filled with specific information—**Safety Alert, Buyer's Guide, Designer Tip, Tool Tip, Time**

Saver, **Homer's Hindsight,** and **Work Smarter** are all there to help you work efficiently and economically. Whenever a project involves something special—whether it's safety or getting the right tool—you'll be prepared for whatever comes up.

AND THERE'S MORE
Introductory information at the beginning of projects will tell you what you need to know. **Real-World Situations** start each section and remind you that the world isn't perfect, so be prepared to deal with issues as they arise. **Tool Kits** at the beginning of Section 2 and 3 show you the basic tools you'll need to do the projects.

GET THE MOST OUT OF YOUR PATIO
To make the best use of what's inside, carefully read through each project before you begin. Mentally walk yourself through the steps from beginning to end until you're comfortable with the process. Understanding the scope of the job will limit unnecessary mistakes and help you avoid spending the money to do things twice.

TAKE YOUR TIME
If you're not a landscaping contractor, don't expect to work like one on your first project. What you'll learn on the job will make it easier as you go along. You'll encounter challenges but will find solutions. Don't be afraid to ask the experts and then listen to what they say. All you need is a willingness to try and a desire to learn.

And don't forget to take a little pride in what you can accomplish with some good advice and a little old-fashioned elbow grease.

Support your local building inspector

Building codes are often confusing to the do-it-yourselfer, but they exist to enforce consistent methods of installation and, more important, to ensure the safety of your family. Sometimes the reason for code is common sense; other times the code may seem silly. However, you must follow codes, so find out what's required and do it from the start. This book is written to meet relevant national codes. But codes change, and local codes can sometimes be more stringent than their national cousins. Legally it's up to you to make sure the job you're doing meets code because the consequences can be serious. Aside from potential danger, an inspector can make you start over (which can get expensive), and you may not be able to sell your house until you fix the violation. Find out what local standards you need to meet and get some advice on how to best go about the job. Get a permit, do the job right, and sleep soundly at night.

Whether you're bracing a post or excavating for a new sidewalk, success is measured by how carefully you've planned for each step of the project.

Some aspects of home improvement can be dangerous, but it's hard to remember that when you're wrestling with a power auger to dig postholes. Being safe in potentially dangerous situations is a way of thinking—and the only way to work.

■ Wear recommended safety gear including gloves, clothing, safety glasses, and ear protection when working with power tools. Flying debris can blind you or distract you long enough to create a disaster. Regular eyeglasses can shatter when hit.

■ Wear a respirator or particle mask that's rated for the job you're doing. Breathing toxic fumes or inhaling particles can have serious consequences.

■ Get in the habit of wearing safety goggles anytime you're working.

■ Always turn off the power at the circuit breaker when working with wiring.

■ Choose the right tool for the job and know how to use it safely.

■ Don't overreach. Move the ladder before you fall.

■ Don't reach above your head to make a cut. Something is bound to fall on you. It may be the cutoff; it may be the saw.

■ Ask questions. Store personnel can recommend the right tools and materials for the job; building inspectors can (and will) make sure you're doing the job right.

■ Take your time. Read the directions carefully, look at the job at hand, and imagine what might go wrong. The surest way to avoid trouble is to be prepared.

BUYER'S GUIDE

FINDING MATERIALS FOR PATIOS AND WALKWAYS

The majority of products and materials used in constructing patios and walkways such as pavers, general building materials, and tools are available throughout the country and are similar size, shape, and quality even though they may be manufactured by different companies. However, some materials are regionally specific and may not be in stock or are simply unavailable in your area. If that's the case, your local home improvement center will work with you to choose substitutes that will meet your needs or they can sometimes special order certain items if they are available and shipping is feasible.

Solid advice and tricks of the trade

Tips, insights, tricks, shortcuts, and even the benefit of 20/20 hindsight from the pros at The Home Depot are worth their weight in gold. Their years of experience translate into instant expertise for you. As you go through this book, look for these special icons, which signal detailed information on a specific topic.

Select the best materials.

HOMER'S **HINDSIGHT**

Avoid common mistakes.

Prevent unsafe situations.

Designer Tip

Design options to change your home.

OOPS!

Fix common mistakes.

Learn shortcuts that work.

Tips and tricks to get the results you want.

Learn what you need to know before you begin.

Preparation and planning save both time and money. The landscaper's golden rule? Don't start digging until you're sure where the patio is going to go.

OUTDOOR DESIGN AND PLANNING

Outdoor spaces serve multiple purposes for you and your family. Well-designed patios and carefully placed walkways are finishing touches that enhance your landscape and add to your quality of life.

Patios are spaces to entertain, to enjoy the garden and the view, and to provide safe play areas for children. Comfortable seating and convenient access to and from the house make patios ideal retreat areas.

Walkways are important considerations in your landscape design. Carefully constructed of materials that are appropriate for your landscape, they become accents and focal points, creating pleasant transitions from one space to another.

This section provides information on the basics of design and planning, offering both design tips and installation examples that succeed as beautiful and functional additions.

Also in this section is information on choosing attractive and durable materials for patios and walkways. You'll learn how to work with these materials and the tools you'll need to install them.

You'll then be introduced to the general concepts of laying out your patio or walkway, the basics of excavation, and an overview of brick and paver patterns.

Design, planning, choosing and working with materials, and effective excavation are all equally important elements in the successful completion of your project.

SECTION 1

REAL-WORLD SITUATIONS

CONSIDER AESTHETICS AND PRACTICALITY AS YOU FINALIZE YOUR DESIGN.

Laying a patio or walkway successfully evolves from careful consideration of several factors:

■ **How will the new patio or walkway fit the existing landscape?** Your home's surroundings should influence the choice of materials. For a formal look, consider brick set in a traditional pattern, such as running bond or herringbone. For informal styles, use natural stone set in random patterns or define an area with gravel or wood chips.

■ **Will the new patio or walkway be part of the public or private spaces surrounding your home?** Public spaces are seen by passersby, and design choices will affect your neighborhood. If possible make choices that complement your neighbors' homes. Private spaces, such as backyards or areas enclosed by fences, offer opportunities to define a more personal style.

■ **Are you confident in your ability to handle both the design and installation of your project?** If you're not sure what you're looking for, consider getting design advice from a landscape designer or seek help from the lawn and garden department of your local home center. Installing patios or walkways may involve working with heavy materials and can be labor intensive. Consider hiring out a portion or all of the labor.

1 DESIGNING A WALK OR PATIO

Designing a patio or walkway requires familiarity with your landscape and a basic understanding of design principles. Together they will help you create outdoor spaces that are both beautiful and functional.

Installing a patio or walkway can be hard work. In many ways, however, coming up with a design that you will be happy with for years is even harder. Find inspiration wherever you can—in books and magazines, garden shows on television, your neighbors' yards, or displays in the garden department of home centers. Once you have some ideas about what you like, start looking at materials and get advice on the advantages and disadvantages of each as well as the complexity of installation.

The following pages will introduce you to basic principles that will help you create a design and develop a plan to carry out to completion.

Elements of design

FORM AND FUNCTION

A successful patio or walkway is a perfect blend of form and function. It is attractive, comfortable, and well-fitted to its site. It is comprised of materials that are in tune with the home and the surrounding landscape. And it is installed to be durable as well as easily maintained. If that sounds like a tall order, it is. Like any other major home improvement projects, you can achieve your goals when you divide the work into manageable pieces and put the puzzle together one piece at a time.

PUTTING THE ELEMENTS TO USE

In this chapter you'll learn how to get started. First you'll learn about the elements of design you'll need to create the right patio for you and your home. They include style, color and texture, pattern and form, scale and visual balance, unity, and variety. You already have some knowledge of these elements. You use them to analyze the objects you like around you every day. Being able to break down what appeals to you by using these elements will help you make wise design decisions.

PAVERS WORK EFFECTIVELY in large spaces because of their uniform size and ease of maintenance. Shrubbery surrounding the patio defines boundaries and the entrance.

THE MORE ACCURATELY YOU MAP OUT YOUR PROPERTY the more successful your final design will be. Sketching on paper helps you think through the concept and will make installation easier.

GET IT DOWN ON PAPER

Make a detailed sketch of your yard to scale, measuring as accurately as you can. Note the position of the house, front yard, backyard, driveway and sidewalks, other buildings, roads, trees, and such landscaping features as shrubbery and garden areas. Photocopy this sketch and use the copies to draft ideas about potential locations for the proposed patio or walkway.

With sketch in hand, find as many sources as possible for inspiration and ideas. Collect pictures and photographs of patios and walkways you like. Gather ideas and let them influence you as you finalize your own design.

Use resources in the garden area of your local home center, where knowledgeable associates and designers will give advice and answer questions. When you spend money to improve your home, foolish questions don't exist.

Elements of design (continued)

THE SIMPLICITY OF THIS PATIO with a central planting space makes it a perfect setting for an abundant and immaculately styled garden.

STYLE

Patio and walkway style has two basic categories—formal and informal. Within the frame of formal and informal are motifs that can be defined as traditional and contemporary.

Formal and informal looks differentiate by how they achieve a sense of style with the use of materials, shapes, lines, and angles. Formal styles use geometry—straight lines, right angles, and geometric shapes. Bricks, pavers, and cut stone all fit well in the formal style. Formal designs also tend to have symmetrical installation: When you draw a line down the middle of a formal patio, the sides are mirror images.

Informal designs are free-form less dependent on geometry, and have pleasing curves and shapes that create asymmetrical balance between elements.

Traditional patio design attempts to control the environment with fountains, courtyards, and columns. Contemporary patios have more daring designs that use opposing materials and shapes, blending into the landscape to make a statement.

WEATHERED BRICK WALLS AND STEPS and a rustic wooden gate enhance the country feeling of this backyard patio. Careful positioning of flowering containers welcomes visitors inside.

COLOR AND TEXTURE

For your patio or walkway, choose colors that complement your home and that appear as part of the natural environment. Warm colors of stone and pavers tend to be red, rust, brown, yellow, beige, and orange. Cool tones include blue, black, and gray. Sand and mortar, which are used to fill joints, also add color to the patio and walkway. The green of grass and mosses that fill the joints of unsanded or unmortared paths offer color as well.

Texture is a matter of both design and safety. Polished materials such as stone or wood have smooth surfaces that can become slick when wet. Use them in enclosed spaces that are not subjected to the elements. The rougher textures of brick, pavers, and natural stone offer solid footing and a natural look. Concrete, the flattest stone surface, can be tinted and textured to make a dynamic design statement.

USING A CONCRETE MOLD ON A WALKWAY to simulate brick adds texture and shape to an otherwise uniform surface. Tinting the concrete adds color.

THE COMBINATION OF WHITE PATIO FURNITURE ON A WARM RED PATIO CREATES AN INVITING OUTDOOR LIVING SPACE. The herringbone pattern of the patio emphasizes the variety of color in the pavers. Invisible edging between the patio and the lawn offers an uninterrupted connection between the two spaces.

Elements of design *(continued)*

PATTERN AND FORM

Pattern and form work together as dynamic patio and walkway design elements. Form refers to the shape of the materials that make up the surface of the patio or walkway. Shapes can be regular, such as brick or pavers, or irregular, such as natural stone.

Pattern refers to the arrangement in which stones are laid. Rectangular pieces, such as brick or pavers, can be laid in a wide variety of patterns—such as running bond or herringbone. Patterns are discussed in this book; you also can create patterns of your own. Patterns can be contained within borders to control visual movement in a space. Forms and patterns can be mixed to create visual interest. Consider mixing various shapes and colors of stone to create a dramatic pattern.

Natural stones have random shapes and are laid together in a free-form manner that creates a flowing, nongeometric design.

THE BORDER OF PAVERS ALONG THE EDGE OF THIS WALKWAY enhances the herringbone layout and is a good example of how opposing patterns can create a sense of order. The border emphasizes the informal curving flow of the path.

THE PERFECT SYMMETRY OF THIS PATIO with equally balanced elements on either side of an imaginary centerline instantly creates a sense of formality and order.

SCALE AND VISUAL BALANCE

Scale refers to how elements of a patio or walkway relate to each other in terms of the overall design. Scale helps define the general feeling of a space.

With the proper use of scale, small areas can be made to feel larger and large spaces more contained. The size, pattern, and type of the materials you choose for your patio or walkway help define scale. Large pieces of stone will emphasize the smallness of a modest space, while smaller stones will seem to fit more easily in the overall scale. Stones of the same size will offer an open and expansive feeling. Varying larger and smaller pieces, either in random pattern or as formal borders in a larger space, will draw attention to the surface and help contain it.

Two basic means achieve visual balance—symmetry and asymmetry. Symmetry occurs when forms of equal visual weight are arranged on each side of an imaginary centerline. Asymmetry creates balance by properly juxtaposing objects that vary in shape, size, and color. Walls or columns of equal height that frame the entrance to a patio or walkway create symmetry. A wall of shrubbery on one side of a patio and a stone wall on the other create an asymmetrical feeling although they can have equal visual weight.

UNITY

As an element of design, unity means harmony. Harmony results in a unified interaction between each element of the design. Your patio or walkway should blend in with your home and the surrounding landscape in a harmonious and pleasing manner. In a unified environment each element is unique but linked to everything else in terms of color, shape, line, and form. A formal 18th-century patio might be at odds with a flat roof contemporary home. A wood chip walkway might seem out of place as the entrance to a formal stone patio.

Unity also rises out of elements that are arranged to lead the eye to a focal point—whether it be the furniture, a wishing well, or a fountain. A well-unified space exudes an inviting and comfortable feeling.

INSETTING ROWS OF BRICK IN THIS SIMPLY POURED SIDEWALK echoes the brick steps and links the sidewalk to the home's entrance level.

VARIETY

Variety is expressed in the use of different shapes, textures, or colors. A perfectly unified space can become predictable without a few elements to surprise and delight. A change in pattern, the addition of a border, interspersing different shapes of stone into an otherwise formal layout, creating a mosaic as a focal point—each adds variety to a unified design.

Alternating squares of different colored stones or using the same stone in different colors as a border both create variety. Including a mix of shapes and textures in the pattern of a stone surface also creates variety.

Proper use of variety allows the eye to continually relive the design and keeps it fresh over time.

MIXING VARIOUS SHAPES, COLORS, AND TEXTURES OF PAVERS offers a means of achieving variety in design. This sunken patio uses three distinct pavers laid in different patterns to create a sense of flow and movement. The border of flowering plants at the base of the wall separates it from the patio and helps define the boundaries of the patio space.

DESIGNING A WALK OR PATIO 13

Practical considerations

INSTALLATION CHOICES

There are three basic types of patio or walkway installation— soft-set, hard-bed, and wood If properly installed, all are attractive and durable.

Soft-set installations are generally easier and faster for homeowners because they don't require a concrete foundation and the joints between the materials are filled with sand. The site is excavated and leveled, then a sand or gravel base is added and compacted. The materials are then laid on the base and the joints are filled with sand. Edging strips are often spiked in place around the perimeter to hold the bricks or pavers in place. Soft-set installations are more prone to shifting due to freeze/thaw cycles and require periodic maintenance. With proper care they will last indefinitely.

Hard-bed installations will last a lifetime because they start with a concrete foundation on which paving materials are laid in a mortar base and the joints are filled with mortar. The resulting patio or walkway is solid and resists shifting and fluctuations due to freeze/thaw cycles. Hard-bed installations are more labor intensive but require less maintenance over time.

Wooden structures in the form of boardwalks or raised decks are -attractive and, if well-maintained, long-lasting.

SITING PATIOS AND WALKWAYS

Access. No matter how perfectly a patio or walkway blends into the surrounding environment, it will receive limited use if access is restricted or difficult. A patio that serves as an outdoor entertaining space will be most effective located off easily accessible living spaces.

Stairs. Stairs transition from one level to another. If your patio is situated on ground that would make a walkway too steep for a straight run or require too many turns in a running path, consider steps or landings at various locations to ease the journey.

Slope. A walkway that is too steep or made of materials that become slippery when wet will limit enjoyment. Locate starting points for walkways that are accessible from the house and that lead directly to an end point. Natural-feeling paths tend to follow the easiest course from the starting point to the end.

SOMETIMES SIMPLE CONCRETE SIDEWALKS ARE THE MOST EFFECTIVE especially when the path passes between two densely-planted flower gardens as shown above. The simplicity of the pathway also helps focuses attention on the ornately styled Victorian porch and home beyond.

Drainage. Improper drainage can leave standing water on a patio, destroying your outdoor experience, the materials that make up the patio, and potentially the foundation of your home. Make sure that the patio slopes away from your home at a rate (approximately 1 inch for every 4 feet) that ensures runoff will be safely carried away.

Site the walkway so that water flows toward a drainage system and not down the path. Gravel or wood chips can wash away on a walkway, following the natural drainage of the terrain. Soft-set stone might be a better alternative.

THE WEATHER AND PATIOS

Sunlight and shade. Hot, bright sun bearing down on brick or stone can make a patio unusable. Too much shade can make it uncomfortable in cool weather. The ideal location for your patio is one that takes advantage of seasonal and daily changes. Locate your patio to make it most effective in terms of how you intend to use it.

PRECAST CONCRETE PAVING SQUARES MOLDED AND TINTED TO RESEMBLE BRICK are used to create a pathway around the side of this house. The sunken path marks a route commonly used by the homeowner's family and saves wear and tear on the lawn.

Orienting a patio toward the east will take advantage of morning light, but the patio will be cooler in the evening, making it a good site for those who enjoy dining outdoors.

West-facing patios will become quite bright and extremely warm in the afternoon unless properly shaded.

Southern sites will receive sun throughout the day and may also require additional shade during warm months. The sun will make the patio more useful during cooler months in areas with extreme climate shifts.

Northern sites receive far less sun and, consequently, will be shadier and cooler throughout the day.

Wind. The wind can either enhance the time you spend on your patio or limit its use. A gentle breeze is a pleasure, but areas with strong wind patterns require some sort of shelter. Select a location that will isolate your patio as much as possible. Patios are often partially or fully covered with roofs or retractable awnings, and some sides are enclosed with either solid walls or glass doors.

Weather extremes. Rain and snow also are factors consider partial roofs or retractable awnings.

The style of your home, weather conditions, and the surrounding terrain are the best guides to the shape and position of your patio or walkway. Walk your property to look for patio sites and interesting routes for walkways. Great views can define a patio site, while the slope and flow of the land will offer insights into the siting of walkways.

Be aware of elements that would create unpleasant views from your patio,

A GRAVEL PATHWAY THROUGH THIS GARDEN echoes the color and weathered texture of the bricks used on the house. A gravel path is easy to install and maintain.

A SUCCESSFUL PATHWAY CAN BE AS SIMPLE as a strip of well-tended grass that connects two sections of a large yard. Create defining borders along the sides with a combination of flowering plants and shrubbery.

Practical considerations *(continued)*

such as a neighbor's compost pile or rickety garage. If an unpleasant vista can't be concealed with fences, walls, or shrubbery, consider another site.

DEFINING PATIOS

Attached. The majority of patios are attached in some way to the main dwelling, usually with easy access from a family area or the kitchen. While one or more of the sides of an attached patio will probably follow the lines of the house, the area that extends into the yard offers the option of free-flowing lines.

Wraparound. Like wraparound porches on Victorian homes, wraparound patios offer access from more than one room of the home. Entrances can be accented or defined with short walls, planters, shrubbery, or lawn furniture. Wraparound patios tend to consume a great deal of square footage, and some zoning ordinances will restrict patio size because of increased water runoff into sewer systems.

Detached. Detached patios should reflect the overall architectural style of the house and its surroundings while taking advantage of views that are not necessarily accessible from the area directly surrounding your home. Detached patios can provide private, secluded settings. Provide access to a detached patio with a walkway that complements its design.

Courtyard. Courtyard patios are defined by the walls that surround them. They are good solutions for both rear and front areas of condos or townhouses. Walls, fences, or plantings can be added to create enclosed spaces. Contemporary homes often revolve around a centrally located courtyard patio that provides access from several points in the house and offers a secluded interior/outdoor space.

DEFINING WALKWAYS

Walkways are generally categorized by their intended use.

Utilitarian walkways are designed to get from one place to another easily and quickly. Although they can be constructed of a variety of materials, from the simplicity of concrete to elaborate paver or brick patterns, their function is to connect exterior spaces in a simple and straightforward manner. Utilitarian walkways should be as level and flat as possible to make movement as easy and efficient as possible. Therefore, they may require excavation and complex installation.

Free-form walkways are about the journey. Often they are sited to follow the natural contours that flow through the property or to simply define a path that has evolved naturally over time. If everyone takes the same route to the beach and the grass is showing signs of wear, it might be time to install stepping-stones or pavers. Consider benches or other seating stationed along the way to invite enjoyment of a particular view. Or concentrate garden elements, such as flowers or shrubs, in delightful spots to create new vistas.

FORM AND FUNCTION ARE COMBINED EFFECTIVELY IN THIS ENTRANCE WALKWAY.
Pavers make up the step and patio surface and slate tiles are laid to create the walkway. Combining elements creates focus and offers a visual reminder of the change in level.

Know the law

If you violate a local code or ordinance when you install your patio or walkway and the local government discovers it, you'll have to alter your design or even its siting to comply. Saying, "Gee, I didn't know," won't get you very far with the inspector, and changes at the last minute can be costly. Factoring in the time involved in doing your project twice, determining what's acceptable before you begin is definitely worth the effort. Another issue to consider is whether deed restrictions that define the limits on what can be installed and what can't are in place in your neighborhood. Do your research before you begin work to ensure that you can enjoy your patio or walkway in peace. Here are some issues to consider as you create your design:

CHECK BUILDING CODES

Building codes exist to protect homeowners from potentially dangerous situations based on faulty construction methods and the use of unsafe materials. They're based on proven industry practices and are approved for safety and uniformity. Know and abide by local and national codes as you prepare to install your patio or walkway. Contact your local building inspector's office for codes that affect your home and property.

RESEARCH ZONING ORDINANCES

Zoning ordinances define how a piece of property can be used and how structures can be placed on it. You usually won't be allowed to put up a gas station in the middle of a residential neighborhood even if it looks like the rest of the houses on the street. Residential zoning ordinances establish minimum setbacks from property lines, utility easements, and possibly size limits of a structure. Information will be available at your county clerk's office or your local government center.

RESPECT DEED RESTRICTIONS

Some communities have adopted deed restrictions in order to maintain control

KNOW THE LOCATION OF BURIED LINES before you begin digging.

over local property values and architectural style. Restraints on the kind of patio or walkway you can build, including the style and the materials you choose, may exist. Some neighborhoods may have unspoken or informal restrictions on the kind of additions that can be installed to maintain the integrity of the neighborhood. While you may not be legally bound to follow these guidelines, it's not fun to be feuding with the neighbors. Take a good look around the area and talk to the neighbors before you install a patio.

CALL BEFORE YOU DIG

Utility and cable companies will visit your site and flag the position of underground lines. Call to have all utilities located before you dig. The placement of underground utility cables, such as electric, communication and telephone, and television, may affect the location of your patio even if the cables are buried deeper than you plan to excavate. Don't restrict access to them unless you're sure you'll never want to change. Sewer, water, and gas lines running to the house must also be considered.

ONCE YOU'VE CREATED YOUR DESIGN review it with a building inspector to make sure you're meeting necessary code and zoning requirements.

2 CHOOSING MATERIALS

OUTDOOR DESIGN AND PLANNING

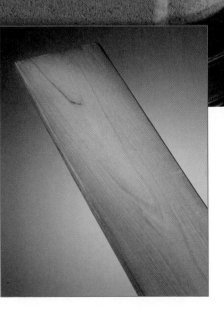

Home centers, landscape suppliers, and lumber yards offer a wide selection of products and materials designed to give your new walkway or patio a personal and distinctive style.

With so many products available, spend time browsing the aisles of the garden department to become familiar with your options as you plan.

When you find a look you like, get advice on the advantages and disadvantages of the product you're interested in as well as the installation of the product.

Ask questions. Get a realistic idea of the complexity of your project so you can be objective about whether to tackle it on your own or hire out some of the work to a professional.

Paver walks and patios

PAVERS

Pavers are different from bricks, though the two often look alike. Bricks are made of clay that has been baked in a kiln until it's hard. Pavers are made of concrete that has been molded into shape. They come in countless shapes and are dyed several different earth tones.

Pavers are the perfect do-it-yourself product. No mortar is needed between the joints, and pavers are laid over a sand-and-gravel bed rather than the concrete pad that mortar requires. In place of mortar, sand is swept into the joints. Most pavers have small tabs on their sides so that the space between them is uniform. Many patterns are available in both full and half pavers, minimizing (but not eliminating) the need to cut them to fit.

A paver walk or patio is really a four-part system: The pavers sit on a 1½-inch layer of sand, which sits on a 4-inch layer of gravel for drainage. The whole formation is held in place by edging, which prevents the pavers from shifting away from each other.

Availability of certain products or materials varies by region. Your local home improvement center can guide you to the right alternative product or, in some cases, arrange for special orders.

THE BEAUTY OF PAVERS IS THEIR UNIFORMITY OF SIZE and consistency of shape, which make installing patios or walkways quicker and easier than when using bricks or natural stone.

SAND AND GRAVEL

You'll want two kinds of sand for a paver walk or patio. Most of the sand you'll need is bedding sand. The pavers sit on a layer of bedding sand, which has sharp edges that won't compact once you bed and compact the pavers into it. The sand that usually goes between individual pavers is mason's sand. It's finer and easier to sweep into the spaces between pavers.

The gravel that goes under the sand should be a gravel approved for use as a bed under asphalt paving. It's a mixture of different sizes of stones that compact and stay compacted so that once in place, the pavers don't settle. (For more on gravel, see page 20.)

Most projects require a large number of pavers, and large numbers of pavers are heavy. You'll also be working with large quantities of sand and gravel. Plan to have the pavers, sand, and gravel delivered. If the job is big, consider hiring someone to excavate and perhaps to put in the sand-and-gravel bed.

COUNTLESS TYPES OF GRAVEL ARE AVAILABLE; THREE ARE SHOWN HERE:
¾-inch gravel (top right), is made of stones that fit through a ¾-inch grid; ¾-inch with fines (top left), is the same gravel with much finer stones mixed in. In between the two gravels is a bagged gravel sold as all-purpose gravel. Underneath walks and patios, use whichever gravel the local road department approves for use under asphalt. Bedding sand (lower left), compacts nicely underneath bricks and pavers. Mason's sand (lower right), is finer and is used in the spaces between bricks and pavers.

Stone

Stone has a variety of shapes, sizes, and textures. Those used in outdoor construction include limestone, sandstone, slate, fieldstone, and granite. Any stone will work, and no one stone is better than another, though some are more expensive than others. In addition to types, stone is sold with types of surfaces: Flagstone has been split into sheets or tiles from thicker slabs; ashlar has been milled into faceted or roughly rectangular blocks; rubble is stone as it's found in the field or as it's blasted out of the quarry.

LIMESTONE is a soft stone that is usually gray or reddish brown. Soft is a relative term in reference to stone. Limestone is plenty hard: The homes that German farmers in Pennsylvania made from limestone in the 1700s are strong and sturdy to this day. Limestone is a sedimentary stone, made of countless shells that formed in huge layers on the sea bottom. You'll often find a small fossil embedded in the surface.

SANDSTONE is formed by a combination of fine quartz particles (sand) bound together by a cementlike calcium carbonate. It is softer than limestone but strong enough to be used in walls and walkways. Colors range from beige to brown and even bluish gray or greenish. Generally speaking, the darker the color, the more durable the stone.

SLATE is clay or shale that has been compressed by the earth above it to form a smooth, abrasion-resistant rock that was once used for blackboards and shingles. Once quarried, slate splits easily into sheets, making it perfect for walkways and patios. You can buy it in sheets up to 2 inches thick for use as a flagstone walk or in thinner, smaller tiles for use on patios.

GRANITE is a volcanic rock packed with particles of quartz. It's the hardest and heaviest of the stones listed here. When milled and highly polished, it is extremely shiny, and it is used for countertops and monuments. In outdoor construction it's seldom given such a shiny finish. It's often milled into semirectangular blocks, however, and used in walls. In areas where granite is common, it is also used in curbs and sidewalks.

FIELDSTONE depends on the field in which it was found. Its chief characteristic is not its content but its shape. In areas that were washed by rivers or glaciers, it may be smooth; in other areas, the surface and edges may be more angular. It's well suited to making walls but is seldom flat enough for walkways.

GRAVEL. Anything between a ¼-inch and a 3-inch stone can be included in a gravel mix. (A ¼-inch stone will pass through a sieve with ¼-inch squares; a 3-inch stone will pass through a sieve with 3-inch squares.) What you want depends on what you're doing with the gravel and you need to be specific.

For a gravel walk, get between ¾- and 1½-inch stones. Larger stones can be difficult to walk on; smaller stones can mush around underfoot like dry sand on

STONE IS USED EITHER AS IT'S FOUND OR AFTER IT HAS BEEN MILLED. Ashlar is a rectangular stone milled for use in walls. Stone tiles (top left), are best used indoors.

the beach and make walking uncomfortable. The grains of gravel are usually jagged, making it easy to compact but uncomfortable to walk on barefoot. River gravel has been washed smooth over time and is more comfortable to walk on barefoot. It does not compact into a smooth surface the way other gravel does, however, and it also may tend to compact underfoot.

If you need gravel for a drainage bed underneath brick, pavers, or concrete, ask for a gravel mix that's approved for use under asphalt pavement. The mix varies from area to area and sometimes from town to town. In simplest terms, the specifications will be something like this: 70 percent of the stones must pass through a ¾-inch grid, 50 percent must pass through a ⅜-inch grid, 35 percent must pass through a No. 4 (12 mm) grid, and so on. Don't worry about the specifics. Just ask for the gravel that the local road department uses.

GRAVEL IS AVAILABLE IN A RANGE OF SIZES to accommodate a variety of needs. Gravel walkways are usually composed of stones between ¾ and 1½ inches.

Grades of brick

To the eye, one brick is much like the next. Sizes vary, some have holes in them, and some are yellow instead of red. If the differences stopped there, you could be sure that whatever you bought would work wherever you put it.

There are, however, two broad categories of bricks—those used as pavers and those used in walls. In addition, each type comes in three categories (SX, MX, and NX), each designed for a different degree of exposure to the weather. All of these bricks look similar, so make sure you tell your retailer what you need.

PAVER BRICKS. You don't want to use a wall brick as a paver: Paver bricks are tougher and designed to resist abrasion. Type III pavers are for home and patio use; Type II is for high-traffic areas, such as stores; Type I is for driveways.

WALL BRICKS. If only a wall brick were just a wall brick, life would be good. But once again you have choices. A face brick has a uniform surface; a hollow brick is a face brick that has large holes running from top to bottom, making it lighter to work with and easier to manufacture. Either is fine for walls. (The exposed top row of a wall will require a face brick.) A building brick has a less than perfect surface and is designed for uses where it won't be seen.

WEATHER RATINGS. Pavers, face bricks, and building bricks all come in three grades based on what their exposure to the weather will be.

SX bricks are for exterior use where the brick is in contact with the ground and may freeze during the winter. MX bricks are for exterior use where freezing does not occur during the winter. NX bricks are for interior use, where the structure shelters the brick from freezing.

WHAT TO GET. What you need depends on where you are and what you're doing. If you're building a patio in Maine, you'll want an SX Type III paver. In Arizona you'll want MX Type III pavers. Wall builders in the North will want SX face or hollow bricks; in the South, look for MX face or hollow bricks.

BRICKS COME IN COUNTLESS SIZES, SHAPES, AND COLORS. Bricks with holes in them are meant for wall construction and are unsuitable for walks and patios. Not all solid bricks, however, are meant for patios or walks. Get a brick called a paver brick, which stands up to wear. Ask for an SX paver brick if you live in an area with severe winters. MX pavers are fine for use in areas with milder winters.

Edge restraints

Edge restraints are an important part of mortarless patios, such as those made of pavers or brick. With no mortar to tie the surface together, every step across the surface pushes the bricks apart. Eventually the bricks or pavers so carefully spaced would inch their way toward the lawn, where there is no base to support them. After that they could settle or roll slightly one way or another. The problem could work its way across the entire patio as the base under the pavers erodes.

Restraints solve the problem and can be almost anything anchored into the ground. Commercially made restraints are usually a plastic strip with a flange that is nailed into the ground with spikes. The restraint isn't as tall as the bricks are high, so the top is invisible once you replace the soil at the edge of the patio or walk. They're the easiest to install and are the least expensive solution.

Other ways to keep your patio from moving include spiking landscape timbers into the ground, setting bricks on end in the gravel bed, or pouring a concrete curb. If the top of the edging will be exposed, it takes planning to ensure it's at the same level as the surface of the walk or patio. A full-size sketch of the edging is a good way to double-check (or avoid doing) the math. It need not be pretty, just accurate. Graph paper with ¼-inch squares eliminates the need for rulers and straightedges. If the edging is of a thickness different from the brick or paver, you have two choices: (1) Dig a stepped bed—a trench along the edges of the bed deep enough to house the edge restraint. The area between the trenches is deep enough for the combined thickness of the gravel drainage bed, the sand bed, and the pavers. (2) Dig a flat bed, put in a gravel bed, then put in the edging. Once the edging is in place, add enough gravel between it to put the pavers at grade.

Typical restraints are shown *below*.

Installing edge restraint alternatives

Timbers: Cut the timbers to fit into the trench, mitering the corners with a chain saw for a perfect fit. Drill ½-inch holes at each end before putting them in the trench. Drive 24-inch lengths of No. 4 (½-inch rebar) into the holes to anchor them into the ground.

Plastic edging: Plastic edging creates an invisible edge around the perimeter of the path or patio. Anchor it by driving 6-inch spikes through the flanges. In some areas of the country it is available in a bendable format to create curves.

Benderboard: Drive stakes on the inside of the curve, then build up the curve with several layers of benderboard. Place stakes every foot on the outside of the curve and where the straight and curved parts meet. Then screw the stakes to the benderboard.

Mortar, concrete, and grout

Concrete, grout, and mortar look much the same, do much the same thing, and come in bags that look pretty much the same. Concrete is used to make sidewalks; mortar holds bricks to each other or to a concrete pad; and grout is put between tiles once the floor is laid. Here's a quick look at what goes into each:

CEMENT is made by grinding up a naturally occurring limestone that contains clay. Portland cement is a stronger manufactured product. It's made by baking cement at 2,700 degrees then pulverizing it. Neither cement is strong enough on its own, and both are mixed with some combination of sand, gravel, and lime to make concrete, mortar, and grout.

CONCRETE is made of cement and fine and coarse aggregates; the fine aggregate is sand and the course aggregate is gravel.

Although concrete is hard, as anyone who has ever scraped a knee knows, it's also brittle. A metal mesh usually runs through the middle of the pad to knit it together if it should ever crack.

MORTAR is a mixture of cement, lime, and sand. Masons often refer to it as an adhesive, but it doesn't come in a bottle or can, and it is neither a glue nor a mastic. It's a cement-based mixture designed to adhere a brick, stone, or paver to a similar object or to a concrete pad.

GROUT is a 1:1 mixture of cement and sand; it also may contain lime. It's finer than mortar in order to create a smooth surface between tiles on a floor or wall. Although similar in content to mortar, the proportions are different, and grout would not work well if you tried to use it as mortar.

Mortar, concrete, and grout are cement-based mixtures. Concrete is used as a pavement; mortar holds bricks, stone, or tile to it. Grout fills in the spaces between the stones.

CEMENT (TOP LEFT), IS A NATURALLY OCCURRING LIMESTONE THAT IS THE BASIS FOR MOST OF THE MIXES USED IN MASONRY. Concrete (top right), is a mixture of cement, sand, and gravel. Grout (bottom left), is made of equal parts of cement and sand and is used to seal between tiles. Mortar (bottom right), is a mixture of cement, lime, and sand and is used to hold brick, stone, and tile in place.

Types of lumber

Most, if not all, lumber used outdoors comes from evergreens. Because evergreens generally tend to be softer than other trees, they are referred to as softwoods. Broad-leaved trees, such as oak, are called hardwoods. Hardwood and softwood, however, are only generalizations: Balsa, for example, is technically a hardwood.

The softwoods used in outdoor construction include cedar, redwood, cypress, and pressure-treated pine. Like all trees, these trees have both heartwood and sapwood. The sapwood is the narrow, lighter-color wood near the bark that completely encases the heartwood. Sapwood is never as strong or rot resistant as the heartwood. Avoid lumber that has lighter strips running along the edges.

PRESSURE-TREATED WOOD has been pressure-impregnated with a liquid preservative. Studies show that once it's in the wood, the preservative stays there, and experience shows the wood lasts longer. Results vary, depending on the wood and the type and amount of the preservative. The best guide comes from manufacturers, who say that pressure-treated wood will last at least eight times longer than untreated wood.

Pressure-treated wood is made from softwoods because softwoods readily absorb the preservatives. Some Western woods are perforated slightly to help the preservative soak in, but most of the wood is Southern pine, which requires no perforation. Because Southern pine includes several types of trees (longleaf pine, shortleaf pine, loblolly pine, and slash pine), the density and strength of pressure-treated wood varies.

Rot-resistance, however, has been standardized. All pressure-treated wood carries a stamp from the American Wood Preserver's Association (AWPA) that indicates the best use for the board based on the amount of preservative in it. Boards for above ground use—such as decking—are stamped "above ground." Boards for use as posts are stamped "ground contact."

As of January 1, 2004, chromium copper arsenate (CCA) is no longer used. The new treatments require the same care when handling the wood, however: Wear a dust mask and safety glasses when cutting the wood, shower when you finish working, and wash the clothes you wore separately from other clothes. Do not burn pressure-treated wood. Put it in the trash or bury it.

REDWOOD grows along the coast of California and produces a wood that is light red to dark brown. It's more easily obtained on the West Coast than on the East, where it is quite expensive. The wood is lightweight, works easily, and is stable. It expands and contracts very little, making it ideal for outdoor use. Heartwood from old-growth trees is highly decay-resistant; second-growth lumber is slightly less so.

CEDAR is found on both the East and West Coasts. Red cedar is dull to bright red with white sapwood. White cedar is light brown with white sapwood. Eastern white cedar is aromatic and is also used in blanket chests and closets. All cedars are rot-resistant and stable and shrink little with changes in weather and humidity levels.

CYPRESS is a Southern wood that comes from the bald cypress, one of two needle-leafed trees that lose their leaves in the winter (the other is the larch). Old-growth cypress is among the most decay-resistant trees and is a favorite for windows, boats, and even caskets. Second-growth cypress is slightly less rot resistant but still a reliable wood for outdoor use. The heartwood is from light yellowish brown to chocolate color. The wood is moderately strong, moderately heavy, and moderately hard.

Grading wood

Lumber is graded although no single grading agency exists, so standards vary from species to species. With any wood, choosing the proper grade is a matter of appearance versus cost. The more you pay, the fewer knots and less sapwood you get. Spend money on what people will see, and use a less expensive grade for posts, joists, or beams. Grading standards for the three most common outdoor softwoods are shown here: Redwood, cedar, and all other softwoods, which includes pressure-treated (PT) wood. Stores often carry a single grade of PT. Visit several and buy from whomever carries the best.

Western red cedar grades

Architect Clear	Stable; defect free; uniform grain
Custom Clear	Stable; a few small knots; grain
Architect Knotty	Stable; wider grain; knots allowed
Custom Knotty	Unstable; has not been dried

Stamp of approval

This representative grading stamp indicates standard-grade dimension lumber of the species Douglas fir with a moisture content of less than 20 percent. A mill's number, as shown here, or its name or symbol identifies the manufacturer. The certification symbol of the Western Wood Products Association means its grading guidelines were used.

Softwood lumber grades

DIMENSIONAL LUMBER (2 to 4 inches thick)

Select	Top grade; defect free
No. 1 (construction)	Few defects; no knots larger than 1½ inches; no checks (cracks at the end of the board), splits, or warps
No. 2 (standard)	More defects than No. 1; may have knots larger than 2 inches or checks; no splits or warps
No. 2 and better	A commonly available mixed grade made of Select No. 1 and No. 2
No. 3 (utility studs)	More defects than No. 2; may have checks, splits, or warps. Used where strength matters and where wood is unlikely to be seen.
Construction	Less strength and shorter span than No. 2 and better
Standard and better	A mix of all the grades above; used in framing

BOARDS (less than 2 inches thick)

Select B and BTR	Highest quality; virtually free of defects or blemishes; expensive and not always available
Select C (choice)	High quality; few defects or blemishes
Select D (quality)	Quality; some defects and blemishes
No. 1 common	Minor defects and blemishes; limited size ranges and not always available

Redwood lumber grades

ARCHITECTURAL GRADES

Clear All Heart	Top grade; contains no sapwood. At least one face is defect free.
Clear	Same as clear all heart, except contains some sapwood
Heart B	Heartwood with some knots
B Grade	Heartwood and sapwood with some knots

GARDEN GRADES

Deck Heart and Construction Heart	Similar grades of pure heartwood; contains knots and some imperfections
Deck Common and Construction Common	Same as deck and construction heart, but contains both heartwood and sapwood
Merchantable Heart	Heartwood with knots, cracks at the end of the board (called checks), and some splits
Merchantable	Same as above but contains sapwood

3 WORKING WITH MATERIALS

Patio and walkway materials are basics of the outdoor construction industry—gravel, dirt, concrete, brick, concrete pavers, stone, and wood. You'll also find such manufactured materials as landscaping fabrics, plastic drainage tubes, steel and plastic edging, rebar, and plumbing and electrical products.

Each product has specific installation requirements and serves a specific design function.

The tools for working with these materials are basic as well: tape measures, hammers, cold chisels, and shovels. You'll also work with power tools, some of which may be unfamiliar to you, such as a dry saw for cutting bricks, a wet saw for cutting tile, and a compactor to compress and level the patio or walkway foundation. Purchase the tools you'll use often; rent the one-time-use tools.

Cutting brick, tile, pavers, and stone

Patio and walkway edges usually have to be cut to fit. You can make the cuts several ways, and the technique is similar regardless of the material. The most inexpensive tool (called a wetsaw) looks like a mini-tablesaw that cuts with a diamond blade bathed in water.

Most pros use a heavier-duty saw that cuts from above, somewhat like a power miter saw. It, too, cuts with a diamond blade that is bathed in water, but it is more powerful than the small version.

Many patterns—such as running bond—start or end each row with a half-brick. A lot of cutting is involved, and often the best way is to make the cuts after the bricks are laid, using a tool called variously a drysaw, cutoff saw, or quicksaw. This saw can be run dry or wet depending on the material you're cutting. When cutting pavers or brick, the drysaw (which is how it will be referred to in this book) is used without water to prevent staining the surface material. Whatever name you choose to call it, the tool looks like a large circular saw but is usually gasoline powered. Guide it along the intended edge of a patio after all the bricks, pavers, or stones are in place.

Power tools make quick work, but hand tools have their place too. They're when when cutting stone which may not fit on a power tool and which looks best with a slightly ragged edge. Each cutting method is covered on the following pages.

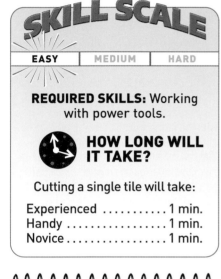

SKILL SCALE

EASY	MEDIUM	HARD

REQUIRED SKILLS: Working with power tools.

HOW LONG WILL IT TAKE?

Cutting a single tile will take:

Experienced	1 min.
Handy	1 min.
Novice	1 min.

STUFF YOU'LL NEED

✔ **MATERIALS:**

Tile

✔ **TOOLS:**

Wet or drysaw, chisels, square, pencil, grease pencil, 3-pound sledgehammer, dust mask, safety glasses, ear protection

To be effective as well as safe, a drysaw needs a sharp blade. Change blades before they get dull to ensure ease of operation and safety.

A DRYSAW SPEEDS INSTALLATION OF PATIOS AND WALKWAYS. Unless you're doing a very large installation, it's probably a good idea to rent the tool. A drysaw operates much like a circular saw, but you need to take some lessons on safety and operation from the rental store and practice with the tool before you start using it for your project.

Cutting brick, tile, pavers, and stone (continued)

USING A TILE SAW THAT CUTS FROM BELOW

1 LAY OUT THE CUT. Saws that cut from below have a limited cutting depth, approximately 1 inch deep, and are generally designed for cutting tile. Draw a layout line with a grease pencil, marking where you want to make the cut. Subtract the width of the joint from the overall size of the tile.

2 MAKE STRAIGHT CUTS. Put water in the tub below the saw. Set the fence so that the layout line on the tile is lined up with the blade. Push the tile into the blade with slow, steady pressure.

3 CUT ANGLES. A miter gauge cuts angles. Loosen the knob and turn the miter gauge until the layout line aligns with the blade. Put the brick, paver, or tile against the angle guide or miter gauge. Tighten the knob to lock in the angle and push the miter gauge forward to cut with slow, steady pressure.

CUTTING WITH A SAW THAT CUTS FROM ABOVE

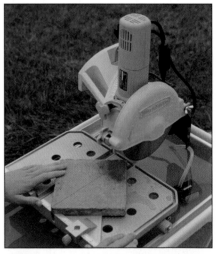

1 LAY OUT THE CUT. An overhead saw makes deep cuts, as much as 3¾ inches. The saws for brick and tile are different, largely because of cutting depth; make sure you rent the one you need. Whichever you have, fill the tub with water. Put the brick, paver, or tile in place and draw a layout line to mark the cut. Subtract the width of the joint from the overall size of the tile.

2 MAKE STRAIGHT CUTS. Add water to the tub below the saw. With the saw off, put the paver, tile, or brick against the lip on the sliding table. Ease the table toward the blade. Align the layout line with the blade and fasten the rip guide next to it. Turn on the saw and push gently and slowly to make the cut.

3 CUT ANGLES. Align the layout line with the blade. Put the miter gauge attachment on the table, set it to match the angle of the brick, paver, or tile, and lock it in place against the material you're cutting. Turn on the saw and feed the table toward the blade to make the cut.

CUTTING PAVERS WITH A DRYSAW

Use a drysaw to cut straight lines or curves after the paving surface is in place. Because you can cut more than one brick, tile, or paver at a time, it's efficient, and as long as you can follow your layout line, you're less likely to make small measurement mistakes.

The saw raises an incredible amount of dust. Make sure to wear a dust mask, close windows to the house, and move cars and items that can be damaged with dust away from the job site. Because of the dust raised, make sure you're cutting to a layout line that is highly visible—bright chalk works well. Spray the line with lacquer before you cut so the dust doesn't erase it as you work. Sweeping and compacting sand into the joints will remove both the lacquer and the chalk.

Wear gloves, a long-sleeve shirt, safety glasses, and a dust mask when operating a drysaw.

1 LAY OUT THE EDGE ON THE GROUND. Snap a line on the ground showing where the paving will end. Lay pavers or brick up to the line. If a paver needs to be trimmed to fit, put it in place without cutting it.

2 LAY OUT THE EDGE ON THE PAVERS. Putting the pavers in place covers the layout line, so lay out the cut on top of the pavers. Spray lacquer on the line to keep it intact as you work.

3 ANGLE THE SAW SLIGHTLY. Most cutoff saws can be run wet or dry. Run it dry so that the combination of dust and water doesn't stain the surface of your work. Start the saw and hold it at a slight angle so the bottom of the paver or brick will be cut a bit shorter than the top.

4 MAKE A FIRST CUT. Guide the saw along the layout line, cutting into the surface. Don't try to make the full cut in a single pass. Let the saw cut as deep as it will go on its own. Cut along the length of the line.

5 MAKE A SECOND CUT. Guide the saw along the first cut, holding it at the same angle and letting it cut as deep as it wants to go. Repeat until you cut entirely through the brick or paver.

Cutting brick, tile, pavers, and stone (continued)

CUTTING BRICK OR FLAGSTONE BY HAND

1 **LAY OUT THE CUT.** Mark the cut line on the material with a pencil or scratch it on the surface with a nail. Make sure the size of the line takes the space between the flagstone or brick into account.

2 **SCORE ALONG THE TOP FACE.** Guide a chisel along the layout line, striking the chisel, moving it, and striking again. To make sure the line is straight, strike the first blow at one edge of the material and the second blow at the opposite edge. Alternate back and forth until the line meets in the middle.

3 **SCORE THE SIDES.** Draw lines on the edges of the material, showing where you want to cut it. Use a straightedge to guide the layout lines. Angle the lines slightly, a bit smaller at the bottom than at the top of the material so it will fit snugly against the edging. Score along the lines.

4 **SCORE THE BACK.** Draw a line on the back, connecting the lines you drew on the sides. Score the line the same way you scored the line on the front of the material.

5 **SPLIT THE MATERIAL.** Put the material you're splitting on the ground, which will absorb the shock. Put the chisel in a score line and strike with a 3-pound sledge. Move the chisel along the line, striking until you split the material.

4 LAYOUT

Laying out the shape and form of your patio or walkway is the first installation step. A layout provides an accurate outline of the outside edges of your patio or walkway project.

Doing an accurate, full-scale layout of the proposed site creates a guide for excavation and ensures that patios that are supposed to be square are square or walkways that curve do so smoothly. The layout also gives you a look at how the design fits in your yard. Is the scale correct? Is the patio in the right place? Does the walkway end at the gazebo? This is your chance to make adjustments before you remove soil.

Considering how important an accurate layout is, it is also the easiest part of a patio or walkway project—it involves no heavy lifting and no digging or dragging. In this chapter are layout basics that will help you lay the groundwork for a successful installation.

Laying out with stakes and mason's line

When builders lay out straight lines, they use stakes and string. Although stakes and string are low-tech, they're almost foolproof: The shortest distance between any two points is always a straight line, even if the points are stakes driven in the ground.

Use 2×2 stakes—they're easier to drive than 2×4s yet large enough so they won't split. When you look for line at the home center, you'll probably find two kinds—the string used for chalk lines, and mason's line. Get mason's line, which is made of nylon and won't sag. A sagging line always creates a problem in layout work, especially when you try to get a reading from a line level hung from it.

SKILL SCALE

EASY	MEDIUM	HARD

REQUIRED SKILLS: Measuring, driving a stake.

HOW LONG WILL IT TAKE?

Experienced	5 min.
Handy	5 min.
Novice	5 min.

STUFF YOU'LL NEED

✔ **MATERIALS:**
Stakes, mason's line, chalk line or powdered chalk

✔ **TOOLS:**
Tape measure, 3-pound sledgehammer, plumb bob, tape

It's easier to remeasure than it is to rebuild. Check measurements early and often.

TWO PEOPLE MAKE LAYING OUT A PATIO OR WALKWAY EASIER AND ULTIMATELY MORE ACCURATE. An accurate layout is probably the most important step in any outdoor construction project. To ensure a good layout, use mason's line instead of string that will stretch and sag, causing problems during installation.

1 LAY OUT A LINE. Drive a stake into the ground a foot or so beyond the space you're laying out. Tie mason's line to the stake, stretch it along the edge you want to lay out, and tie it to another stake. Drive the second stake into the ground a foot beyond the length you're laying out. If the line is supposed to be a specific distance from a structure, measure several places along the line before you drive the stake.

2 LAY OUT A PERPENDICULAR LINE. Stretch a second line between stakes as you did for the first line. Before you drive the second of these stakes, square up the first and second lines with a framing square.

3 **DOUBLE-CHECK FOR SQUARE.** Double-check the layout with the 3-4-5 triangle method. (See page 38.) Put pieces of tape 3 feet from the corner of one line and 4 feet from the corner of the other line. If the lines are square, the distance between the pieces of tape will be 5 feet.

4 **MAKE ADJUSTMENTS.** If the distance between the pieces of tape is a measurement other than 5 feet, move a stake to make adjustments. Pull it out of the ground and wrap the line around it several times so you won't drive the stake near the first hole. Have a helper measure between the pieces of tape. Drive in the stake when the measurements confirm the lines are square.

5 **MARK THE CORNER ON THE GROUND.** Transfer the corner formed by the lines to the ground with the help of a plumb bob. Hang the plumb bob at the intersection of the lines. Mark the ground with a nail driven through a piece of paper.

6 **DRAW A LINE ON THE GROUND.** For a precise line between two points, snap a chalk line on the ground, choosing a color that's easy to see. For a general line, sprinkle chalk powder, flour, or lime along the mason's line.

Laying out with batterboards and mason's line

Another means of laying out a patio is to use batterboards made from 2×4s and mason's line. By sliding the line along the horizontal bar of the batterboard, you'll be able to bring the sides into square. Batterboards are positioned 1 or 2 feet outside the area for the patio so they don't get in the way of excavation.

When you work with batterboards, make sure they're level with each other. If they are, the lines are also level, and you can measure from them to determine the slope of the ground and the slope of the surface that results from digging.

SKILL SCALE

EASY	**MEDIUM**	HARD

REQUIRED SKILLS:
Measuring, leveling, driving batterboards.

HOW LONG WILL IT TAKE?

Laying out an 8×10-foot patio will take:

Experienced . . . . 1 hr.
Handy . . . . 1.5 hrs.
Novice . . . . 2 hrs.

STUFF YOU'LL NEED

✔ **MATERIALS:**
2×4s, 2×2s, mason's line, 10d (3-inch) common nails, masking tape, powdered chalk

✔ **TOOLS:**
Tape measure, circular saw, hammer, plumb bob, 3-pound sledgehammer, line level, garden hose, safety glasses

LAYING OUT STRAIGHT EDGES

1 **BUILD THE BATTERBOARDS.** Build two batterboards for each corner you lay out. Cut points on two 2-foot-long 2×4s. Then nail a 2×4 crosspiece between them a couple of inches below the top.

2 **POSITION THE BATTERBOARDS.** Drive a pair of batterboards at right angles to each other a foot or so beyond where you estimate each corner will be.

3 **WHEN YOU LAY OUT A PATIO OR WALKWAY NEXT TO A HOUSE,** drive a nail into the siding to mark one corner of the excavation. If the patio or walk will follow the length of the house, drive a second nail in the siding at the opposite end, positioning it with a line level so that it's level with the first nail.

A+ WORK SMARTER

BATTERBOARDS RULE
It's difficult to understate the importance of an accurate layout. The success of the entire project hinges on how carefully you set up the outline for a patio or walkway. Batterboards may seem like extra work, but the advantage is that they will stay securely in place and, if firmly pounded in place, they won't move while you're pulling lines taut or making the inevitable adjustments to ensure 90-degree angles at corners. Batterboards also can be stored and reused, so it's really worth the extra time involved in knocking them together. In the long run they'll save you time, and frustration.

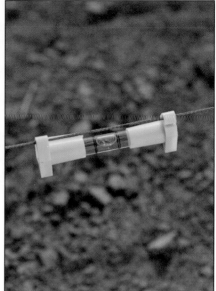

④ TIE MASON'S LINE TO THE CROSSPIECES. Run line between the batterboards to lay out the approximate sides of the excavation. If the patio butts against the house, run line to the nails you drove into the siding.

⑤ LEVEL THE LINES. Hook a line level onto a line. Level the line by driving a batterboard farther into the ground. Repeat on adjacent sides until all four sides are level with each other.

⑥ SQUARE A CORNER. At one of the corners formed by the lines (use the house as one of the sides, if possible), check for square with the 3-4-5 method: Mark one line 3 feet from the corner with a piece of tape. Mark the adjacent line 4 feet from the corner. The corner is square when the distance between pieces of tape is 5 feet. Slide the line along the batterboard, if necessary, until the lines are square. (See page 38 for more information.)

⑦ SQUARE A NEIGHBORING CORNER. Square neighboring corners with the 3-4-5 method. If you have to reposition one of the lines, move one other than the one that was used to create the first corner.

Laying out with batterboards and mason's line

LAYING OUT STRAIGHT EDGES (continued)

8 **LAY OUT THE REMAINING SIDE.** On the top of the batterboards, mark the desired length of the patio on two parallel lines with masking tape. Run mason's line between the batterboards so that the line crosses the pieces of tape on the two sides. Check both corners for square with the 3-4-5 method.

9 **DOUBLE-CHECK FOR SQUARE.** Check the entire layout for square by measuring diagonally across the area from opposite corners. The length of the diagonals should be equal. If not, repeat Steps 6 to 8.

10 **MARK THE CORNERS ON THE GROUND.** Once all the corners are square, drop a plumb bob from each and use chalk to mark the patio corners on the ground. Mark the batterboards to show the location of the strings.

HOMER'S HINDSIGHT

TRUST THE PROCESS

People ask me why I'm always saying, "Don't take shortcuts." The reason is simple: Take the time to do each phase correctly, and you'll end up with a job you're proud of. A lot of steps may not seem important at the time, but they all have a purpose. Over the years masons and landscape contractors have learned a lot about how to guarantee success with their installations, and following time-tested procedures only makes sense. In the long run the benefits of following through with each step in the process will far outweigh what may seem like extra effort at the moment. Stick with the plan—it'll save you headaches.

LAYING OUT A SLOPE

Drainage in the form of a slight slope away from the home is essential to keep water away from the foundation of the house and to keep standing water from building up on the patio surface. Patios should slope away from the house a minimum of ⅛ inch every foot. Very wet climates require a slope of ¼ inch every foot. Check local building codes to find out what's required where you live.

Lay out the slope with stakes and mason's line to help you excavate at the right slope. Start with a level batterboard layout, as explained on pages 34–35. Then drive stakes, stretch lines between them below the lines on the batterboards, and measure to create the proper slope.

Once you lay out the slope, drive in more stakes at 6-foot intervals. Stretch line between them to lay out a grid that you can use to check the excavation depth.

1 DRIVE TWO STAKES AT EACH CORNER. Drive a 2×2 stake between each batterboard and the chalk mark at the patio corner. Use a plumb bob to make sure the lines still cross over the chalk mark.

The right slope will ensure proper drainage. Standing water on a patio is no fun.

2 STRETCH LINE BETWEEN THE STAKES. Run mason's line between the stakes. For now, the lines on the stakes should be parallel to and below the lines on the batterboards. Measure down from the line on the batterboards and slide the line up and down the stakes until the distance between the lines is the same at each corner. Use a plumb bob to make sure the lines cross over the chalk mark.

3 LOWER THE LINES. To lay out the slope of the patio, lower the lines on the stakes farthest from the house by a minimum of ⅛ inch per foot. (Check to see what's required locally.) With a ⅛-inch slope, the outside edge of an 8-foot patio would be 1 inch lower than the edge at the house, for example. Mark the desired drop distance on the corner stakes farthest from the house, then lower the lines to the mark.

4 CREATE A GRID. Mark where the lines meet the batterboards and remove the lines, leaving the batterboards. Drive stakes every 4 feet along the patio outline. Run lines between the stakes to lay out the grid. The grid will make it easy for you to excavate the area to the proper depth later by providing frequent reference points.

5 MEASURE AS YOU DIG. Dig trenches along edges and grid lines. Measure to make sure the bottom of the trench and the lines are the same distance apart along the entire length of each. Then excavate between the trenches, using a level and a 2×4 to make sure the patio is level from side to side.

Laying out perpendicular sides

There's really no tool made to square up two sides of a patio. The framing square, which comes closest to being useful, is too small and often inaccurate. The Greek master of geometry, Pythagoras, devised a theorem for verifying perpendicularity that builders still use today.

THE 3-4-5 TRIANGLE

If one side of a triangle is 3 feet long, the other side is 4 feet long, and the distance between them is 5 feet, then the sides meet at 90 degrees and are square.

If you're interested in the theory, it's the Pythagorean theorem, which says that for a triangle with two sides at 90 degrees to each other, the square of the hypotenuse is equal to the sum of the squares of the sides: $5 \times 5 = (3 \times 3) + (4 \times 4)$.

If you're not interested in the reason, it simply works. If you want to know whether two lines form a 90-degree angle, measure 3 feet from the corner on one side and 4 feet from the corner on the other. If the distance between the two points is 5 feet, the sides are square.

The 3-4-5 triangle works whether you measure in inches, feet, yards, or miles. It also works with any unit of measure in the metric system and with multiples of three, four, and five. A 6-8-10 triangle has two sides at 90 degrees, as does a 9-12-15 triangle. In inches, it may help to know that a triangle with sides that measure 1½ inches, 2 inches, and 5 inches is square.

A helper will make any layout easier and less frustrating. You can do it on your own, but as with most endeavors, two is faster and more fun than one.

RECHECK MEASUREMENTS FREQUENTLY AND MAKE ADJUSTMENTS AS NECESSARY. Make sure you and your partner agree on how you are reading the tape measure as you do the layout.

SKILL SCALE

EASY	MEDIUM	HARD

REQUIRED SKILLS: Measuring, basic carpentry.

HOW LONG WILL IT TAKE?

Setting up batterboards and squaring lines for an 8x10-foot patio will take about:

Experienced . . . . 1hr.
Handy . . . . 1.5 hrs.
Novice . . . . 2 hrs.

STUFF YOU'LL NEED

✔ **MATERIALS:**

2×4s for batterboards, mason's line, masking tape

✔ **TOOLS:**

Tape measure, framing square

Squaring a square

Framing squares are usually close to accurate, but dropping them or letting them bang around in the back of a truck can knock them out of alignment. Check with a multiple of the 3-4-5 triangle. The distance between the 12-inch mark on the short arm and the 16-inch mark on the long arm should be 20 inches. It's close enough if the measurement is within 1/16 inch.

Bring an out-of-square tool back in line by judiciously using a hammer. If the measurement is less than 20, tap with a ball peen hammer on the inside corner of the square. If the measurement is more than 20, tap on the outside corner.

① SET UP BATTERBOARDS FOR ONE SIDE. At least one side of any structure is usually laid out in relation to an existing structure—a house, a patio, or the property line. Measure from the existing structure and set up batterboards and line to mark the location of the new structure.

② SET UP BATTERBOARDS FOR A SECOND SIDE. Put batterboards and line in place to approximate the location of the second side. Measure from any structure, if distance from it is important. Slide the line perpendicular to the first.

③ MEASURE 3 FEET ALONG ONE LINE. Begin at the point where the lines cross and measure 3 feet along either of the lines. Mark the line with masking tape at this point.

④ MEASURE 4 FEET ALONG THE SECOND LINE. Go back to the intersection of the lines. Measure 4 feet along the second line and mark the spot with a piece of tape.

⑤ CHECK DIAGONAL. Measure between the pieces of tape. The distance will be 5 feet if the lines are perpendicular to each other. If the measurement is anything other than 5 feet, reposition one of the lines.

⑥ SLIDE THE LINE AND RECHECK. You can slide either of the lines along the batterboard. If one line is supposed to be a fixed distance from a structure, then slide the other one. Slide the line until the distance between the pieces of tape is 5 feet, or square.

Checking for level and plumb

You'll find that it's almost impossible to build anything without using a level or transit, described later. Patios, walls, walks—all need to either be level or slope at a controlled rate.

Level is a measurement from side to side: A level object has no slope in any direction. In addition to checking whether an object is level, a level will also check whether it's plumb. Plumb is a measurement from top to bottom: A plumb object is straight up and down.

Levels are available in two broad categories—the standard level is a spirit level, and reading it depends on centering a bubble in a vial. A water level is based on the fact that when water is put in a flexible tube, it settles to the same height at each end. Because this holds true for tubes 25, 50, or even hundreds of feet long, a water level is perfect for checking whether widely separated objects (such as fence posts) are level with each other.

The shorter a level, the less accurate it's likely to be. The levels contained in the handle of combination squares are the least reliable—not necessarily

because they're poorly made but because it's entirely possible that the level is sitting on the only section of the surface that is level. A 9-inch torpedo level is good for checking an 8- to 12-inch-wide surface for level, but for most construction, a 4-foot level is best. A 3-foot level is the shortest you should use. Longer levels are likely to be too awkward in most situations.

Before you buy a level, put it on a flat surface and check the reading. Then turn it end for end and make sure you get the same reading. Finally, turn it over so that what was the top edge is now the bottom, and check the reading again. If the readings are different at any point along the way, the level is either warped or the vials are misaligned. Get another level. Once you have a level that gives you an accurate reading, repeat the process to check whether the level accurately measures for plumb.

You can increase the effective length of a level by resting it on a straightedge and checking the surface with the straightedge. Make sure, however, that your straightedge is truly straight— 8-foot 2×4s, for example, are notoriously

warped. You'll know the 2×4 (or other straightedge) is straight if no gap appears when you put it against another straightedge.

Line levels, which hang from mason's line used for layout, are an exception to the relationship between length and reliability. For all practical purposes, the level is as long as the line it hangs from. Make sure you use mason's line; regular string will sag and throw off the reading.

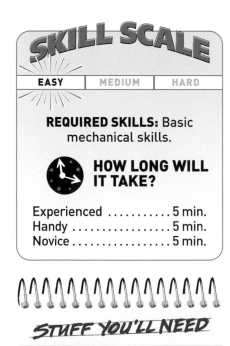

SKILL SCALE

EASY	MEDIUM	HARD

REQUIRED SKILLS: Basic mechanical skills.

HOW LONG WILL IT TAKE?

Experienced . . . . 5 min.
Handy . . . . 5 min.
Novice . . . . 5 min.

STUFF YOU'LL NEED

✔ **MATERIALS:**
Straightedge (such as a 2×4)

✔ **TOOLS:**
Level, line level, post level, or water level

USING A STANDARD LEVEL

1 PUT THE LEVEL ON A FLAT SURFACE and look at the vial in the middle of the level. If the surface is level, the bubble will be centered between the lines, as shown.

2 IF THE SURFACE ISN'T LEVEL, LIFT THE LOW END. The bubble will always slide up the vial toward the high end of the surface. To see how far out of level something is, lift the low end of the level until the bubble centers between the lines. The space between the bottom of the level and the surface is the amount the surface is out of level.

USING A LINE LEVEL

A LINE LEVEL HOOKS ONTO A MASON'S LINE and is used to level a line for layout. Use mason's line, which will not stretch and will give you an accurate reading. The line is level when the bubble is centered in the vial. Raise or lower an end, as needed, to bring the line into alignment.

Checking for plumb

Put the level flat against a vertical surface. The surface is plumb if the bubbles in the vials toward the end of the level are centered between the lines. The object shown here is out of plumb. To see how far it's out, lift one end away from the surface until the bubble centers between the lines. The amount of gap between the edge of the level and the surface is the amount the surface is out of plumb.

PLUMBING A POST

A POST SHOULD BE PLUMB IN ALL DIRECTIONS. Check it with a post level, which slips over a corner of the post and gives readings from both faces.

USING AN ELECTRONIC WATER LEVEL

1 FILL THE TUBE WITH WATER. Attach one end of the tube to the measuring unit. Measure the amount of water recommended by the manufacturer into a container. Put the free end of the tube in the water (dyed red in the photo to make it easier to see). Keep the end attached to the measuring unit at a point somewhere below the container. Suck on the tube attached to the unit to fill the tube. Tighten the clamps to trap the water in the tube.

2 PUT THE MEASURING UNIT AT THE DESIRED HEIGHT. Once it's in place, loosen the clamps. Take the free end of the tube to the object you want to check, temporarily keeping the free end below the end attached to the unit.

3 LIFT THE FREE END UNTIL THE UNIT BEEPS. When the unit beeps, the water at the free end of the tube is at the same height as the water in the measuring unit. Points that are even with the water at each end are level with each other.

Using a builder's level

Landscapers—who have bigger projects, and more of them, than average do-it-yourselfers—lay out the shape and grade of their projects with a builder's level. It's a simple tool to master, accurate, quick to use, and available at most rental centers. Unless you lay out work frequently, renting is more economical than buying.

A builder's level is often called a transit, even by those who ought to know better. The scope on a builder's level turns from side to side. A transit has a scope that can be angled up and down as well as turned from side to side—a feature you don't need for patios and walks. A builder's level is also less expensive to rent and less confusing to use.

The design of a builder's level varies by manufacturer and model. One level may have three wheels that level the scope; another may have four wheels. The small level used to level the tripod may be a tube or it may be a small circle. Make sure you get an owner's manual when you rent so you know what and how to adjust. Once you get started, the use of the level is the same no matter which one you have.

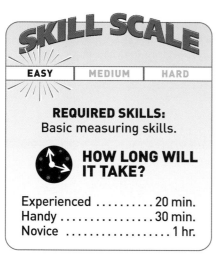

SKILL SCALE

EASY	MEDIUM	HARD

REQUIRED SKILLS:
Basic measuring skills.

HOW LONG WILL IT TAKE?

Experienced . . . . 20 min.
Handy . . . . 30 min.
Novice . . . . 1 hr.

STUFF YOU'LL NEED

✔ **MATERIALS:**
Batterboards, stakes, mason's line

✔ **TOOLS:**
Builder's level, leveling rod, tape
measure, plumb bob, tape

Make sure the legs of the tripod are planted firmly on the ground. If the level moves or shifts, you'll need to start over.

IT PAYS TO BE ACCURATE when you lay out the slope of a patio or walkway. A builder's level is a quick and easy way to ensure accuracy.

1 **LAY OUT ONE SIDE OF THE EXCAVATION.** Lay out one side of the excavation with batterboards and mason's line. Put the batterboards about a foot past the end of the excavation. Measure along the mason's line and put pieces of tape on the line to mark the corners of the excavation. Put landscape spikes below the tape with the help of a plumb bob.

2 **POSITION THE TRIPOD OVER THE FIRST CORNER.** Center the tripod over the spike with the help of a plumb bob. Set the tripod firmly on the ground at one of the corners of the excavation facing the middle of the excavation. Level the tripod by adjusting the length of the legs. Attach the builder's level, and turn up the leveling screws as far as they will go.

3 **LEVEL THE SCOPE.** Turn the telescopic sight so it's directly over two of the leveling wheels. Turn one of the wheels to center the bubble as best you can in the level next to the scope. Then turn the scope clockwise so one end is over one of the first two wheels and the other end is over the third wheel. Level as before and turn the scope clockwise until it is centered over the third wheel and the first. Check for level and adjust by turning one of the wheels until the bubble is centered in the dome.

4 **CALIBRATE THE SCOPE.** Have a helper stand at the second corner with the leveling rod. Turn the scope until you've centered the rod in the crosshairs. Turn the ring to read 0.

5 **LAY OUT THE THIRD CORNER.** Turn the scope until the indicator reads 90. Have a helper with a tape measure and leveling rod step in front of the scope and walk far enough away to be at the third corner. Double-check the distance, make sure the rod is plumb and centered in the crosshairs, and mark the location of the third corner.

6 **LAY OUT THE FOURTH CORNER.** Turn the scope toward the fourth corner until you get a 45-degree reading. Have your helper measure from the corner just marked to the point where the tape indicates distance enough away to be at the fourth corner. Have your helper move in the crosshairs. Double-check the measurements and crosshairs, and mark the fourth corner.

Using a builder's level (continued)

LAYING OUT THE GRADE

1 **SET UP THE BUILDER'S LEVEL.** Put the level near the middle of the excavation. Level both the tripod and the scope.

2 **DRIVE STAKES AROUND THE EXCAVATION.** Drive stakes every 4 feet about 12 inches beyond the edge of the excavation.

3 **FIND THE HIGH END.** Have your helper stand next to a stake at the high end of the excavation while holding the leveling rod. Turn the scope so you can see the rod, and note the measurement in the crosshairs. Repeat at the other stakes at the high end. The stake with the smallest measurement is the highest stake.

4 **MARK THE FIRST STAKE.** Have your helper stand next to the high stake with the telescoping leveling rod. Mark the rod with a piece of tape to indicate the reading in the crosshairs. Then make a mark on the high stake to show where it meets the 6-inch line on the leveling rod.

5 **MARK THE SECOND STAKE.** Have two helpers stand at another stake along the high side of the excavation and lift the stick off the ground until the tape marker is in the crosshairs. Mark the stake at the 6-inch mark. The marks on the two stakes are now at the same level. Repeat for all the stakes at the high end.

6 **MARK THE LOW END.** Without moving the tape marker, repeat the process for the stakes at the lower end. These marks are level with each other and those at the high end. Measure down at the low end by the amount you want the patio to slope ($\frac{1}{8}$ to $\frac{1}{4}$ inch per foot). Make a second mark, as shown in the inset. Snap chalk lines between this mark and the mark on the corresponding stake at the upper end, and mark any stakes in between.

5 EXCAVATING

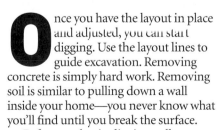

Once you have the layout in place and adjusted, you can start digging. Use the layout lines to guide excavation. Removing concrete is simply hard work. Removing soil is similar to pulling down a wall inside your home—you never know what you'll find until you break the surface.

Before you begin digging, call to arrange for all the utilities to be located and marked. Gas, electrical, cable, and phone lines may be buried close to the surface, and cutting or damaging the

utilities can be dangerous and expensive to repair. A rock or a tree root may slow your progress because removing either one can be challenging and time-consuming.

While working take your time and listen to your body—take breaks frequently, wear the right clothes and gloves, use the right tools, and lift with your legs instead of your back. A pulled muscle will slow you down more than taking a few pauses in the action to rest.

Removing old concrete

SKILL SCALE

EASY | **MEDIUM** | HARD

REQUIRED SKILLS:
Handling a jackhammer.

HOW LONG WILL IT TAKE?

Removing an 8×8-foot concrete slab should take about:

Experienced .... 5 hrs.
Handy .... 6.5 hrs.
Novice .... 8 hrs.

STUFF YOU'LL NEED

✔ **MATERIALS:**

None

✔ **TOOLS:**

Jackhammer with chipping and cutting bits, safety glasses, dust respirator, work gloves, ear protection, wheelbarrow

WORK SMARTER

GETTING RID OF THE DEBRIS

Concrete is heavy and results in a lot of weight and jagged pieces when it's broken up. Use a jackhammer to break the concrete into manageable chunks that won't strain your back when you load them into a wheelbarrow or pickup. Be reasonable when loading a wheelbarrow or pickup and do not overload it.

The old concrete can be used as landfill if you need to fill a hole or build up a berm. It also can be disposed of at a municipal waste facility for a fee.

Check with local codes to make sure you are aware of the restrictions on disposal in your community.

A JACKHAMMER MAKES SHORT WORK OF DEMOLISHING A CONCRETE PAD, but it's noisy and provides a real workout. Take the time to learn how to use it and follow all safety instructions.

If an existing concrete pad is sound, you can often put a brick, stone, or paver patio on it. But cracks, holes, flaking, or an uneven surface are problems that will eventually work their way through a new surface. A new crack will eventually reappear right above the old one no matter how much repair work you do in advance.

To correct problems between control joints—lines cut through the surface at regular intervals when the concrete is wet—you may be able to limit the concrete taken out to the area between the joints. If not you'll have to remove the entire surface.

Removing concrete is just plain hard work, and you may want to hire someone to do it. To do it yourself plan to rent a jackhammer, at the very least, and have a plan to get rid of the broken-up material.

Jackhammers are simple to operate, and electric models don't require the expense, noise, and bother of big compressors required for pneumatic hammers. Technically, jackhammers are demolition hammers. (Chipping hammers are smaller and designed for work on walls and concrete ceilings. Rotary hammers are smaller yet and are little more than drills that twist as they pound.) Rent a 40- to 50-pound electric demolition hammer and let the weight of the tool do the work.

The biggest problem you're likely to face in removing concrete is the wire mesh that runs midway through the slab, which is put in as the concrete is poured in order to tie the concrete together. You'll have to cut through it with the hammer in order to break the concrete into manageable chunks.

The power of a jackhammer will initially surprise you. Hold on firmly and let the tool do the work. Consider a back brace if you're doing a large amount of demolition.

OPERATING A JACKHAMMER

1 **PUT THE TIP IN THE HAMMER.** Make sure the hammer is unplugged. Swing the retaining arm back toward the handle. Put the cold chisel tool or the cutting point in the socket and swing the arm back in place. The cutting point usually works best when pounding through an old surface.

2 **PUT THE HAMMER ON THE SURFACE.** Plug in the tool and put the cutting edge near an edge or near the damaged area of the surface you want to remove. Most tools have a "no load" striking safety that keeps the hammer from running unless it's on a surface. You may have to push down firmly on the tool to start its motion.

3 **BREAK UP THE CONCRETE.** Let the weight of the tool do the work—trying to push on it will wear you out without getting the job done any sooner. Move across the surface, breaking it and creating new cracks as you go. Follow the cracks with the jackhammer to break up the concrete more quickly. About 2 inches into the pad, you'll run into the wire reinforcing mesh. Cut through it with the jackhammer, switching to a wider tip, if necessary, to break the concrete into manageable pieces.

4 **HAUL AWAY THE RUBBLE.** Disposal of the rubble will be your hardest job. You can use it as clean fill somewhere in your lot or have it hauled away on a truck. Load the rubble into a wheelbarrow and haul away.

SAFETY ⬢ ALERT

A jackhammer is designed to demolish material, so treat it with respect. Wear a dust mask to keep the dust out of your lungs and goggles to protect your eyes. Wear ear protection to shield your ears from the noise.

Don't operate a jackhammer in the rain or on a wet surface. Not only is the surface slippery, the water may damage the tool or cause an electrical shock. Make sure you will not be cutting through live electrical wires or conduit.

Use only an extension cord rated for outdoor use and one that is rated to handle the amperage drawn by the hammer. Plug the machine into a properly installed GFCI to lessen the possibility of shock.

Excavating for a walk or patio

SKILL SCALE

EASY | **MEDIUM** | HARD

REQUIRED SKILLS:
Basic mechanical skills.

HOW LONG WILL IT TAKE?

Excavating an 8×10-foot patio should take about:

Experienced . . . . 5 hrs.
Handy . . . . 7 hrs.
Novice . . . . 9 hrs.

STUFF YOU'LL NEED

✔ **MATERIALS:**
2×4s, mason's line, powdered chalk

✔ **TOOLS:**
Garden edger, sod lifter, mattock, spade, shovel, 4-foot level, straightedge, gloves

Excavation simply means digging. Use the right tools to make the job as efficient as possible. A garden edger quickly cuts a straight line through sod. A shovel with a curved blade is for digging; don't confuse it with a spade, which has a flat back and is designed to cut the edge of a trench. To remove sod, break up the surface with a mattock, which looks like a pick. If your patio is large, you might want to use a sod lifter, which has a curved handle and will save you much bending. When excavating, make sure you dig out all roots and organic material, which tend to decay, collapse, and undermine your patio. The depth you dig depends on the type of patio: 8 to 9 inches for bricks or pavers set on a sand-and-gravel base, 8 to 9 inches for a concrete slab patio, and 11 to 12 inches for bricks or stones set in mortar on a concrete slab.

WORK SMARTER

HOW TO USE A MATTOCK

In small areas, rolling up the sod can be a quick way to remove it. If you're excavating for a large patio, however, it may be easier to break up the sod and toss it in the wheelbarrow with the rest of the dirt. The tool to use for this job is a flattened pick called a mattock. Let the tool do the work. Swing the blade up, bring it downward with some force but loosen your grip slightly, and let it hit the ground under its own steam. You'll get "mattock elbow" if you try to slam the tool into the ground. Medically speaking, it's the same as tennis elbow and it hurts.

SAFETY ALERT

Check for any septic system, gas, water, phone, cable, and electrical lines before digging.

1 **LAY OUT THE SHAPE.** Set up batterboards and use mason's line to lay out the outline of the patio or walkway. Use powdered chalk to mark the outline.

2 **STEP ON THE EDGER TO CUT STRAIGHT INTO THE SOD.** Work your way along the layout lines. To remove wide areas of sod, cut 1-foot strips with the edger. Lift the sod with a shovel or sod remover. Hold the blade at a low angle. Put weight on the top of the tool to cut between the soil and the roots and pry it loose.

3 **REMOVE THE SOD FROM THE EXCAVATION.** Roll the sod and remove it from the area to be excavated. Put at least some of it in a cool, shady place and use it to patch the lawn when you finish the project.

④ DIG A TRENCH. Work along the layout lines, measuring down from them to dig a trench to the desired depth of the excavation. Usually the excavation slopes as it runs away from the house and is level from side to side. The directions for individual projects state the proper slope. Dig the trenches at the recommended slope.

⑤ CHECK WITH A LEVEL. Rest a level on a straightedge and check to see if the trench is level. If the excavation is supposed to slope for drainage, put a wedge between the straightedge and the level equal to the desired slope over the length of the level.

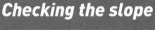

Checking the slope

Patios and walks should slope away from the house so they don't channel rain toward the foundation. The typical slope is ⅛ inch to ¼ inch per foot, depending on rainfall; ask your local building officials for the required slope in your area. Check the slope by propping a wedge underneath one end of a level.

If the slope should be ¼ inch per foot, for example, the wedge would be ¼ × 3 or ¾ inch thick on a 3-foot level. It would be 4 × ¼ or 1 inch thick on a 4-foot level.

⑥ DIG BETWEEN THE TRENCHES. Large excavations, such as those for patios, will have a grid of layout lines, and you should dig a properly sloped trench under each one. Once you have, dig out the space between the trenches. Smooth by pulling a 2×4 along the surface and check with a level, as in Step 5. Regrade as needed and compact.

Crowning a walk

SKILL SCALE

EASY	**MEDIUM**	HARD

REQUIRED SKILLS:
Measuring, excavation.

HOW LONG WILL IT TAKE?

Experienced . . . . .Variable
Handy . . . . .Variable
Novice . . . . .Variable

VARIABLES:
Creating a crown is a variation on the way you screed the walk bed. It lengthens the job by 5 to 10 minutes.

STUFF YOU'LL NEED

✔ MATERIALS:
Bedding sand or mortar, walk materials

✔ TOOLS:
Batterboards, mason's line, line level, tape measure, level, shovel, screed, jigsaw, wheelbarrow or tarp to hold excavated materials, safety glasses, work gloves

Walks, like patios, should be sloped ⅛ to ¼ inch per foot. But rain running down the slope can turn the ground where it empties into a swamp. Mortar walks are more of a problem because they are essentially sealed while sand-based walks provide a little more natural drainage. Crowning is generally required in mortar walks but it's a good idea to crown sand-based walks as well. The crown is acheived by using a curved screed in which the center is higher than the edges so water can flow off to the sides as well as down the slope.

Cut a gentle curve in the screed board so that the center of the walk is about 1 inch higher than the edges.

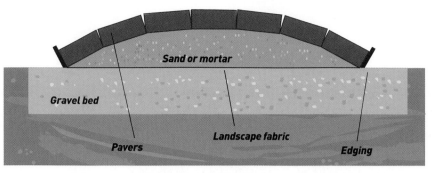

Sand or mortar

Gravel bed

Pavers

Landscape fabric

Edging

A SLIGHT CROWN IN THE CENTER OF A PAVER WALKWAY provides additional drainage by allowing water to flow off the sides as well as down the slope. (The curve in the illustration above is exaggerated for effect.) A mortared walk does not require landscape fabric between the gravel bed and the mortar but you will need to use fabric on a sand-based walk.

A+ WORK SMARTER

CROWING A MORTAR-BASED WALK

To install a mortar-based walk follow basic procedures until you pour the concrete:
- Layout the walk
- Excavate the path
- Build the forms
- Put down a gravel bed if required

- Pour the concrete (The concrete should be poured to slightly overfill the forms so that you can screed the curve into the mixture).
- Screed and proceed with laying the brick

1 LAY OUT THE WALK. Lay out a level bed: Drive batterboards about a foot outside the edges of the walk, connect them with mason's line, and attach a line level. Drive the batterboards into the ground so the line between each set of batterboards is level, and square up the lines with a 3-4-5 triangle. (See page 39.)

2 LAY OUT THE SLOPE. Even though the surface will be crowned, it needs to slope downhill away from the house. The standard slope is ¼ inch per foot, so the low end of an 8-foot walk should be 2 inches below the upper end (8 × ¼ = 2). Drive stakes as explained in "Laying Out a Slope," page 37. Measure down to the top of the grade on the upper stakes. On the lower stakes measure down an equal amount plus the slope. Slide the layout lines down to meet the marks.

3 **EXCAVATE.** Dig for the walk section by section, digging first below the lines and making sure that the distance between the lines and the ground is constant. Excavate the area in between to create a flat surface. Mark where the lines meet the stakes, and remove the lines to put in the bedding sand. Then put the lines back in so you can get the right slope. Compact the sand to form a flat surface. Put the edge restraints in place.

4 **CUT A CURVE IN THE SCREED.** To crown the surface of a walk, lay out a curve on the screed. Mark 1 inch from the edge at the center of the screed.

5 **LAY OUT THE CURVE.** Drive a nail in the screed at the mark. Have a helper flex a thin piece of wood—such as a yardstick or the strip of tempered hardboard shown here—so that it curves from the nail to the bottom corners of the screed. Trace along the piece of wood with a pencil to lay out the curve. Cut along the line with a jigsaw.

6 **SCREED THE SURFACE.** Put the screed along the guides set for it. In some cases you'll be able to use the edge restraints; in others simply follow the line you stretched to mark the grade.

Installing outdoor drainage systems

Many yards have low spots that fill with water. Sometimes a new patio or walk will actually create the problem: Water doesn't soak through the new surface, running into the yard and puddling instead. Seepage trenches will solve the problem. Dig a trench at the low point of the problem area, line it with either flexible or rigid drainpipe, and channel the water away from the house and away from the neighbors. If you have nowhere to divert the water, run the pipe to a dry well, an underground pit filled with stone. The water will collect there and percolate into the ground.

SKILL SCALE

| EASY | **MEDIUM** | HARD |

REQUIRED SKILLS:
Basic mechanical skills.

HOW LONG WILL IT TAKE?

Installing a 10-foot-long trench with a dry well should take about:

Experienced .... 4 hrs.
Handy .... 6 hrs.
Novice .... 8 hrs.

STUFF YOU'LL NEED

✔ **MATERIALS:**
Gravel, 4-inch perforated drainpipe, pipe couplings, sod, landscape fabric, concrete or patio blocks

✔ **TOOLS:**
Round-edge shovel, level, spade, scissors, work gloves

CONSTRUCTING A DRY WELL

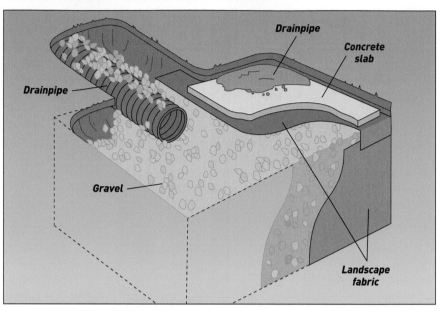

Drainpipe
Concrete slab
Drainpipe
Gravel
Landscape fabric

A SEEPAGE TRENCH OR DRAIN USUALLY RUNS DOWNHILL to exit the ground, but it can also drain into a dry well. Put the low end of your seepage trench a minimum of 10 feet from the house. If you dig a dry well, cover the inside of it with landscape fabric and fill the hole with gravel. The landscape fabric keeps the soil from mixing with the gravel. Cover the dry well with a patio block to keep rain from seeping into it. Cover the patio block with soil and sod.

1 **DIG A TRENCH FOR THE PIPE.** Dig a 2-foot-wide trench about 6 inches deep for the pipe along the entire length of the low edge of the trouble spot. Continue in a straight line to a point where the pipe can exit the ground or to where you'll dig for the dry well.

2 **SLOPE THE BOTTOM OF THE TRENCH.** Dig to create a slope of ⅛ inch for every foot of trench length. To gauge the slope, slip a ½-inch spacer between a 4-foot level and a straight 2×4 that is at least 4 feet long. When the bubble in the level is centered, you have the right slope.

3 **DIG THE DRY WELL.** If the water will drain into a dry well, pick a spot in line with the ditch you're digging, at least 10 feet away and downhill from the house. Dig a hole 2 to 4 feet wide and about 3 feet deep. Make sure to avoid buried cables or utility lines. If you suspect that surprises lurk underground, call local authorities and have them flag locations.

4 **PUT IN GRAVEL AND A DRAINAGE PIPE.** Shovel in enough gravel to cover the bottom of the trench. Lay 4-inch-diameter drainpipe along the bottom of the trench. (With rigid pipe, which has a single row of holes, lay the holes facing down.) Continue running pipe to where the pipe leaves the ground or a few inches into the dry well. If you need to connect lengths of pipe, do it with fittings and without glue.

5 **LINE EACH SIDE OF THE DRY WELL WITH LANDSCAPE FABRIC.** If the water is to drain into a dry well, line the well with landscape fabric, using a large enough piece to extend over the top layer of gravel (Step 7). The landscape fabric keeps soil from mixing with the gravel. Cut a hole in the landscape fabric for the drainpipe.

6 **COVER THE PIPE WITH GRAVEL.** Shovel enough gravel into the trench to cover the pipe. Lay landscape fabric over the gravel. Fill the rest of the trench with soil and cover the soil with sod or seed.

7 **FILL THE WELL WITH GRAVEL,** leaving enough room at the top for a patio block cover, a topping of 2 to 3 inches of soil, and a layer of sod. Fold the ends of the landscape fabric over the gravel.

8 **COVER THE TOP.** Place a layer of gravel over the landscape fabric. Place a large concrete patio block on top of the gravel to keep water from entering through the top. Cover the patio block with 2 to 3 inches of soil and a layer of sod.

Installing outdoor drainage systems *(continued)*

BUILDING A BERM TO DIVERT WATER

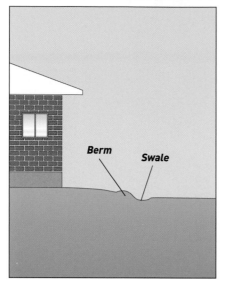

A BERM IS A SMALL EARTHEN BARRIER that redirects the flow of water. It's usually paired with a shallow ditch, called a swale, which helps drain away the water.

1 **REMOVE THE SOD.** Use an edger to sever a strip of sod as wide as a shovel. Pull up the sod and set it aside.

2 **BUILD UP THE SURFACE.** With a wheelbarrow, spade, and rake, spread topsoil along the strip of bare ground. Tamp and smooth the soil to create a small mound. Cover the mound with the sod you removed.

DIGGING A SWALE TO CARRY WATER

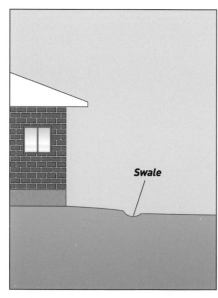

SWALES ARE SHALLOW TRENCHES that catch water and channel it away from the house and toward a more suitable spot, such as a storm sewer. The swale should run along the bottom of the slope to catch water and drain it away. Allow the swale to follow the natural slope of the land.

1 **REMOVE THE SOD WITH AN EDGER.** Then dig a trench as wide as your shovel and about 2 inches deep. Drive in two 2×2 stakes, stretch mason's line between them, and level it with a line level. On the low end of the swale, lower the line ¼ inch for every foot that the swale is long.

2 **DIG TO CREATE A SLOPED SWALE.** Work your way along the swale, digging to keep the bottom a constant distance from the line. After digging, mound and compact the earth on the downhill side of the trench. Cover the trench with the sod you removed.

BRICK AND PAVER PATTERNS

Bricks have always been major players for patios and walkways, and pavers in a variety of shapes, sizes, and colors have become popular in recent years. Pavers are cast concrete and are durable, consistent in size and thickness, and easy to lay either as hard-bed or soft-set installations. Some pavers interlock to create a distinctive pattern.

In this chapter you'll learn about several of the most common layout patterns for bricks and pavers, including the traditional running bond, offset bond, basket weave, 45-degree herringbone, and 90-degree herringbone, and the basics of installation. You'll refer back to these pages when you're actually laying out your pattern for your patio or walkway project.

Square pavers or tiles that are designed for outdoor use can be installed in diamond or 90-degree patterns similar to ceramic tile patterns in your home.

Laying a running bond pattern

LAYING BRICKS IS SIMILAR TO LAYING PAVERS, except you need to pay more attention to spacing and alignment. Running bond is one of the simplest patterns to create. Every second row begins with a half brick, offsetting the joints from row to row.

1 **STRETCH A GUIDELINE.** Put a brick at the beginning and end of the first course. Stretch a line along the edges of the brick as a guide, anchoring the line with another brick, as shown.

SAFETY ALERT

Always wear safety goggles and work gloves when cutting brick and pavers.

2 **LAY ROWS OF BRICKS.** Lay a row of bricks or pavers. If they have no tab on the edges to space them, cut thin pieces of plywood to use as spacers. Embed the bricks in the sand with a rubber mallet. Start the next row with a half brick to stagger the joints. Alternate, starting one row with a full brick and the next with a half brick. Check for high or low spots with a 2×4 and add sand or tap bricks in place as necessary.

3 **TRIM BRICKS TO FIT.** To cut a brick, score a line around the entire brick with a brick chisel and a 3-pound sledgehammer. Position the brick chisel in the scored line, then snap off the extra length with the sledgehammer.

4 **FILL THE JOINTS WITH SAND.** Once all the bricks are laid, sweep a layer of fine sand, often sold as mason's sand, over the walk with a broom or stiff brush to pack the joints between the bricks.

5 **COMPACT THE SURFACE.** Compact the entire surface with a power tamper. Some manufacturers recommend that you spray the surface with water to wash and fill the sand into the joints.

Laying a basket-weave pattern

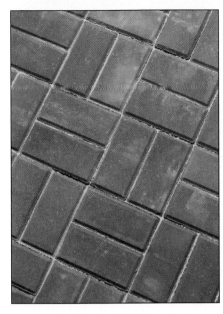

BASKET-WEAVE PATTERNS require no cutting if you plan the borders correctly. Start in the middle of an edge and lay three short rows to create a stepped pyramid. Once the rows are laid, work diagonally, filling in the steps until you cover the surface.

1 **SNAP A LINE DOWN THE MIDDLE.** Lay out the patio or walk and put the edge restraints in place. Snap a chalk line down the center of the sand bed.

2 **BEGIN LAYOUT AT THE CENTER LINE.** Put the first brick in place against the edging, with the long edge on the centerline. Make sure it's square. Lay six bricks on each side of the line in the pattern shown.

3 **LAY THE SECOND ROW.** Begin the second row before you finish the first. Starting at the centerline, place the bricks following the pattern, laying only four bricks on each side of the line.

4 **LAY THE THIRD ROW.** Install two bricks on each side of the line to create a stepped pyramid pattern. From now on you'll lay bricks in the steps, which will keep the bricks aligned and square.

5 **FOLLOW THE PATTERN.** Start at the edge restraints and nestle two bricks in the corner created by the restraints and the bricks already laid. Work your way up the stepped sides of the pyramid on each side. Continue laying in a stepped pattern to lay the entire surface. Cut end pavers as needed to fit against the restraints.

Laying a herringbone pattern

HERRINGBONE IS FANCIER THAN RUNNING BOND but no harder to lay. It is, however, more time-consuming because so many bricks need to be cut. The finished effect is eye-catching, and many do-it-yourselfers feel the result is well worth the trouble. Measure to make sure you get the right size of brick: The true (rather than the nominal) length of the brick must be twice the true width for the pattern to work.

1 **START IN A CORNER.** Lay out the walk or patio as shown in Chapter 4, Layout. (See page 31.) Lay out a trial run along each edge to make sure the bricks or pavers fit and adjust the borders if necessary. Starting at one corner, lay a pair of full bricks at right angles.

2 **CONTINUE ALONG THE EDGE WITH HALF PAVERS OR BRICKS.** Install a pair of half bricks next to the full pavers in the corners, as shown, and begin laying a leg of full bricks in the stepped pattern. Spread piles of pavers along the path so you don't have to make trips back and forth as you lay the pattern.

3 **LAY BRICKS DIAGONALLY.** Lay a leg of full-length bricks or pavers in a stepped pattern, as shown. Once a leg is properly laid, bed the bricks in the sand with a tap from a rubber mallet.

4 **END THE FIRST DIAGONAL LEG AND START THE NEXT.** End the first leg with a half brick. Then lay another stepped leg of full bricks.

5 **CONTINUE LAYING STEPPED LEGS,** finishing each end of every other leg with a half brick. After the walk is laid, sweep sand in between the bricks. Then compact the walk with a power tamper to embed the bricks and spread the sand between the joints.

Laying diagonal herringbone

DIAGONAL HERRINGBONE is a more complicated pattern to lay. It involves cutting numerous bricks or pavers to fit. Lay the pattern using full bricks, then make all the cuts to fill in at the edges. Measure carefully for the location of the starter row and check your work constantly as you proceed.

1 LAY A SMALL SAMPLE. Lay nine pavers as shown. To make sure the layout is square, draw a line at a 45-degree angle across one brick, as shown, and connect the corners of the other bricks in a straight line. Measure the distance between the two lines. Stretch a mason's line this distance from the edge.

2 LAY THE FIRST FOUR BRICKS. Make sure the line you stretched in Step 1 is parallel to the edge restraints; reposition if necessary. Lay two bricks, as shown, so that the outside corner of one and the inside corner of the other fall along the line. Lay two more and make sure they are square.

3 LAY A STARTER ROW. Snug two bricks up against the first bricks, aligning the corners as in Step 2. Follow the line all the way across the surface you're covering.

4 LAY SINGLE ROWS. The next row and all subsequent rows are single rows. Align them by tucking the second brick of the row in place. Next lay the first brick of the row, then lay the remaining bricks in the row.

5 CHECK AGAINST A STRAIGHTEDGE. Lay two rows, then stretch a line across the surface. The corners of each block should just touch the line. If not, adjust the bricks so that they do. Continue laying rows and checking the alignment until the surface is covered with whole bricks. Cut bricks to fill in the spaces at the edges of the pattern.

Laying octagonal pavers

OCTAGONAL PAVERS ARE REALLY KEY SHAPES. A square extends from the octagon. These are difficult pavers to lay, and laying them involves much trimming. To fit them use the open field method, in which you put in the edge restraints on two sides and cut the pavers to fit them. On the other two sides, lay all the stones, cut a straight line in them while they're on the ground, then install the restraints against the pavers. Brick pavers are often installed between the pavers and the edge restraints as a border.

1 LAY OUT CUTS ON THE FIRST TWO PAVERS. Put edging on two adjacent sides of the patio or walkway and mark the other sides with layout lines. Some manufacturers make half pavers that simplify trimming. If you can't get them, lay out cuts on two pavers. To lay out the first cut, lay a straightedge along the side of the square extension and draw a line across the octagon. Put the straightedge on the second paver so that it connects the bottom chamfers of the pavers, and draw a line.

2 PUT THE PAVERS IN THE CORNER. Cut the pavers along the layout lines. Put them next to each other in the corner of the installation.

Using a drysaw to cut bricks or pavers takes a little practice. Take some trial runs to get the hang of it before you make cuts on your pavers.

3 LAY OUT AND CUT THE SECOND ROW. From now on all the pavers will be laid diagonally. Trim the first paver of the second row and put it in place. Lay full pavers next, working diagonally across the patio or walkway until you lay the last paver of the diagonal, shown here.

4 LAY THE THIRD ROW. Begin the third row with a trimmed paver and work diagonally to the other edge. Trim the last paver to fit. Continue laying diagonal rows until you have filled the patio or walkway and reach the layout lines along the other side. You should have no empty spaces along the layout lines, and parts of some pavers will extend across them.

5 CUT TO FIT. Snap chalk lines on the surface of the pavers to mark the edges of the paved surface. Cut along the lines with a drysaw. Remove the scraps and install the border, if any. Then install the edge restraints.

Laying multiweave pavers

Multiweave pavers have zigzag edges. The pavers nestle perfectly against one another, making installation easier; however, they can be hard to check against layout lines, and the shape requires some extra cutting. Most manufacturers sell half pavers that you can use instead of cutting your own. It's worth figuring out how many you'll need.

Any pattern that will work for rectangular pavers will work for multiweave pavers, and once installed the zig-zag edges make the pattern appear more intricate than it actually is.

Because of all the cutting involved, multiweave patterns are a perfect candidate for the open field method: Install edging on two adjacent sides and lay the pavers so that each one either meets or goes past your layout lines. Rent a concrete saw with a diamond blade, snap new layout lines, and cut along them with the saw. (For more on the open field method, see page 72.)

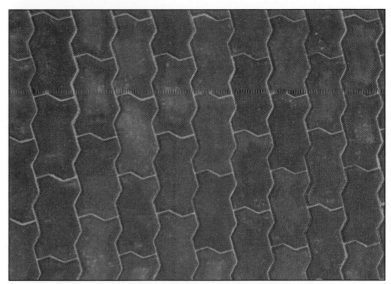

RUNNING BOND. Laying this pattern will be simple if you put a border on the edges perpendicular to the long side of the bricks. Once you have, start the pattern with one of the half pavers sold separately with most multiweave pavers. Then lay full bricks against the border, completing the first row. Install the second brick of the second row, then cut the first brick to fit.

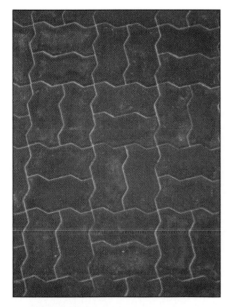

BASKET WEAVE. Like basket weave with other bricks, the trick to successful layout is to plan so that the total size of the walk or patio is an exact multiple of the paver size. Measure the overall size, which includes the face of the brick and the tabs along the side that keep the pavers a constant distance apart.

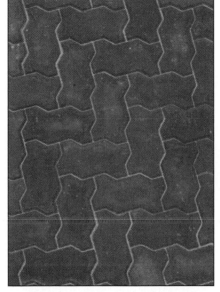

ALTERNATE BASKET-WEAVE PATTERN. This is another pattern in which the walk or the patio should be a multiple of the size of the paver. If it's anything less, you'll have to do a lot of trimming to get the blocks to fit along the edge.

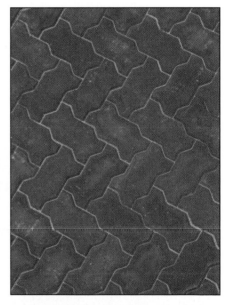

DIAGONAL HERRINGBONE IS ANOTHER CANDIDATE for the open field method, in which you put in only two adjoining edge restraints. (If you put in all four restraints at the outset, expect to cut at odd angles to get the pavers to fit.) To lay an open field walk or patio, start laying at the restraints. Lay the entire surface, continuing up to the lines marking the unrestrained edges. Then cut along the lines using a drysaw and install the edge restraints.

WALKWAYS

Three basic types of installation for walkways exist—soft-set, hard-bed, and boardwalks. Each type offers an attractive, functional, and durable landscape solution, and each has its own needs for installation and care.

Soft-set walkways are composed of stone laid over a foundation of level, compacted sand. They are the easiest to install because they don't require a concrete slab base and the joints are not mortared. A soft-set walkway can have a rustic and natural quality when crushed gravel or wood chips are spread to outline a path.

Hard-bed walkways start with a concrete base. In its simplest form a hard-bed walkway is the familiar poured concrete sidewalk. More decorative options are those in which stones, bricks, or pavers are laid on a concrete slab or foundation and the joints between the stones are mortared for strength. They are more labor intensive to install; however, they require less maintenance than soft-set walkways.

Boardwalks are good solutions in places with irregular terrain, such as wooded or wetland areas, or as access to a lake or beach. They are essentially narrow decks with or without railings and are constructed like long decks. Boardwalks can be mounted on posts set in concrete or on concrete piers. They also can rest on concrete bases set along the route of the path.

In this section you'll find specific information on each of the three types of walkway installations and a chapter on installing rustic pathways.

SECTION 2

REAL-WORLD SITUATIONS

IT'S ABOUT THE LOOK, BUT IT'S ALSO ABOUT THE TERRAIN.

Choosing the right walkway for your landscape certainly involves how the design and materials will complement your landscape. It also involves how effectively your choice can be installed and maintained in the existing terrain. A hard-bed walkway without terracing or connecting steps may not be the best choice in a hilly area or one with a steep slope. It may also require extensive excavation to level and set the foundation. Conversely, soft-set walkways can be more easily adapted to existing conditions, meandering over the landscape and following natural pathways. Boardwalks adapt to almost any terrain, but they can be an intrusion in the environment.

The choice of style and materials also depends on how the walkway will be used. Soft-set stones may have high aesthetic appeal but might not hold up effectively in areas of heavy traffic, such as a driveway or a section where drainage is a constant problem. If all you're looking for is easy access to a utility area, such as a garage or storage shed, a poured concrete sidewalk might be the best choice.

As you make your decisions, consider labor required to install the materials, and maintenance. Be objective and willing to consider other solutions.

WALKWAYS TOOL KIT

3-POUND SLEDGEHAMMER	**COLD CHISEL**	**DRUM ROLLER**	**MASON'S LINE**	**POWER MITER**	**SHOVEL AND SPADE**
BRICK CHISEL	**COMBINATION SQUARE**	**FLOOR ROLLER**	**MASON'S TROWEL**	**POWER TAMPER**	**SPEED SQUARE**
BROOM	**CONCAVE JOINTER**	**FRAMING SQUARE**	**MATTOCK**	**RATCHET AND SOCKET SET**	**STRAIGHTEDGE**
BUCKET	**DARBY**	**HAND TAMPER**	**PAINTBRUSH**	**RUBBER MALLET**	**TIN SNIPS**
CHALK LINE	**DRILL AND BITS**	**LEVELS**	**PLUMB BOB**	**SAFETY GLASSES AND DUST MASK**	**WET SAW**
CIRCULAR SAW	**DRY SAW**	**MASON'S HOE**	**POSTHOLE DIGGER**	**SCREW GUN, COUNTERSINK BIT**	**WHEELBARROW**

WALKWAYS

Aggregates

Some pathways can be built directly on the ground, but most sit on either a sand-and-gravel bed or a concrete slab.

If you're working on a sand-and-gravel bed, you'll quickly discover that it's impossible to just buy some sand or just buy some gravel. Each comes in several varieties, depending on the size and shape of the components. Here's a guide to what's what:

GRAVEL. Often called coarse aggregate, gravel is made of granules of different size. The quarry actually sifts them to give you gravel with uniform pebble size. It also mixes them together to get a mixture with certain characteristics. What you want depends on what you're doing.

If you're building a gravel walk, get gravel with pebbles that are between ¾ and 1 inch long. Smaller pebbles feel too much like walking on sand; larger ones create a surface that's irregular and difficult to walk on.

For a drainage bed under either concrete or sand and pavers, you'll want gravel with a mixture of different grains. The specifications call for mixtures in a given proportion of seven different grains that range in size from 2 inches to .0029 inch. The mixture is designed both to compact and to drain well. Fortunately you don't need to remember the recipe. Ask for gravel that your state or county uses as a "dense graded aggregate base material under flexible asphalt pavement." It's exactly what you want.

SAND. Often called fine aggregate, sand is graded with different-size and different-shape particles.

Bedding sand is the sand you put on top of gravel as a surface for pavers. Like gravel, it's made of a complex recipe of seven different-size particles, designed to compact well. The particles are smaller than gravel, of course, ranging from ⅜ inch to .005 inch.

Mason's sand is the sand to use when filling in the small spaces between pavers. Bedding sand will work, but mason's sand is finer, and will fill the spaces more quickly and with less settling.

CONCRETE, MORTAR, AND GROUT.

Concrete is a mixture of sand, gravel, and portland cement, used to create strong patios, foundations, and floors.

Mortar is a mixture of cement and sand (or cement, sand, and lime), used to glue one piece of masonry to another. Masons call it "mud"; those who write textbooks call it "adhesive." It's most often seen between masonry in a brick, stone, or concrete wall. It's also used to attach brick, tile, or stone to a concrete pad. It may contain a latex mixture, or polymer, that makes it less prone to cracking.

Grout is similar to mortar except that it is made with a finer sand. It, too, may contain a latex polymer.

Aggregates (from top left): **A** ¾- inch gravel with fines (a mixture of finer sands), **B** ¾- inch gravel, **C** concrete, **D** mortar, **E** grout, **F** bedding sand, (G) mason's sand.

Pavers and bricks

PAVERS

The difference between pavers and bricks is a simple one: A paver is made of precast concrete. A brick is made of kiln-fired clay. Neither is inherently better than the other: The compressive strength, abrasion resistance, and freeze/thaw resistance of each are comparable.

Pavers come in a wider variety of shapes; bricks come in a wider variety of sizes. Bricks can be laid on either a sand-and-gravel bed or a concrete pad. Pavers can, too, though the vast majority of installations are over sand and gravel.

Pavers designed for residential use are usually $2\frac{3}{8}$ inches thick. Pavers designed for streets, airport, and port use are $3\frac{1}{8}$ inch thick. Both have small ribs, called spacer bars or nibs, on the side; these automatically create the proper spacing when two pavers are put side by side.

The paver walks in this book are all installed over a sand-and-gravel base. Edge restraints hold the walks together, while sand swept between the pavers keeps them from moving around within the restraints. A rectangular paver stays in place better than a square one.

Spacer ribs **A** ensure that pavers will be the proper distance apart when laid side-by-side. Residential pavers **B** are thinner than pavers **C** used in commercial applications where heavy traffic will affect durability.

BRICKS

The greatest concern when buying bricks is that you buy a brick made for the local climate. SX bricks are designed for areas with freezing and thawing in the winter; MX bricks are for winters in areas that don't freeze over. NX bricks are for interior use and don't belong on a walk or patio.

You also want to get bricks that are specified as paver bricks. Construction bricks, meant for use in walls, are not as abrasion resistant.

Finally, you need to specify how the brick will be used. In the world of bricks, the three bricks shown here are all the same nominal size—$4 \times 1\frac{1}{2} \times 8$ inches—but the actual size has been adjusted to account for the thickness of the joint.

The bottom brick **A** is for paving over a sand-and-gravel base. It is smaller than its name size by the thickness of a joint—$\frac{1}{8}$ inch. The spacer bars help ensure accurate spacing, and the chamfered edges keep you from tripping over a slightly out-of-level brick. The middle brick **B** is also called a $4 \times 1\frac{1}{2} \times 8$ brick but is smaller than each dimension by $\frac{3}{8}$ inch. When put in a walk or patio with $\frac{3}{8}$-inch mortar joints, the brick will combine with the mortar to take up the full $4 \times 1\frac{1}{2} \times 8$ inches for which it is named. The brick on the top of the pile **C** is yet another $4 \times 1\frac{1}{2} \times 8$-inch brick. It's smaller than it's name by a full $\frac{1}{2}$ inch and is meant to be used in masonry with $\frac{1}{2}$-inch joints.

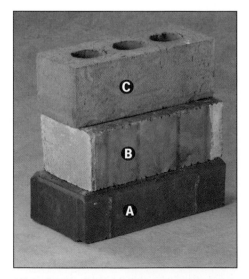

All the bricks above are the same nominal size but their actual measurements are adjusted depending on how they will be used.

Edging

Edging is an important part of any paver walk, or any other walk set on a sand-and-gravel bed. The pavers, sand, and gravel combine to give you a firm, well-drained surface, but without edging, the surface wouldn't stay put. Use, abuse, and weather slowly would push the pavers apart. Eventually the pavers would have enough room to tip and tilt, and in a few years the surface would resemble rubble more than a walk. Edging locks the pavers in place, and the sand between the joints combines with the pavers to make a rigid, durable surface.

Walk edgers fall into two groups: those that work by themselves and those that need extra anchoring. Avoid garden edging designed to keep grass away from flower beds; it is not strong enough to contain the materials used in a walkway.

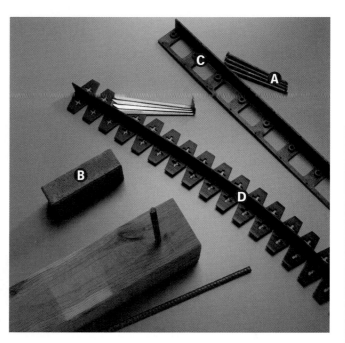

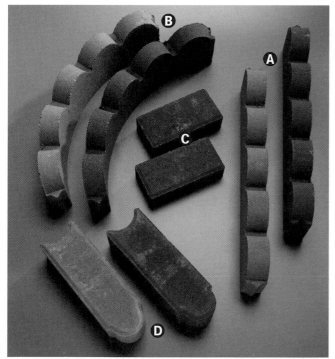

In order to stay put, precast concrete edging needs to be as tall as the combined thickness of the sand, gravel, and paver. Use shorter edging like that shown here to dress up the edges of your walk, but anchor it firmly with another edging. Polyethylene is a good choice. **A Scalloped edging** is designed primarily for use around gardens but can also be used along sidewalks. **B Curved edging** can be used along the edge of a curved walk if the radius is right. **C Edger blocks** can be laid in a straight line or curve. **D Contrasting pavers,** or pavers put at a right angle to those in the pattern, look like edging but are really a pattern variation that needs to be anchored by some other type of edging.

Some types of edging work well in the lawn but aren't strong enough to hold pavers in place. Among the edgings that won't work with pavers are edgings like **A Black polyethylene** which is designed to be an edging between the lawn and garden.

Some types of edging are strong enough that all you need to do is anchor them into the ground. **A Landscape ties,** for example, need only be held in place with landscape spikes. Use ties that are a minimum of 6×6; smaller lumber is likely to warp. **B Bricks** can be put on end in a trench alongside the walk to hold the pavers in place. Commercially-made polyethylene is one of the most popular edgings. Use **C rigid polyethylene** for straight runs and **D flexible polyethylene** for curves. (Flexible polyethylene is not available in all regions. Consult with your local home improvement center for a suitable alternative.) Both are designed so that when installed, they come only partway up the side of the paver. When you finish the walk and fill in around it, the edging is hidden underground, held in place by metal stakes.

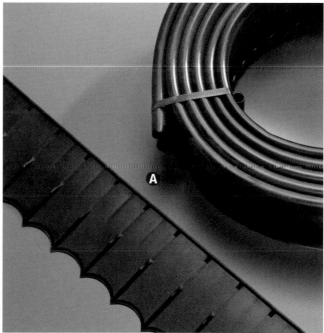

Paver patterns

All walks may be built the same, but not all walks are identical. What a walk looks like depends less on what it's made of and more on its pattern. The walks on the next few pages use simple patterns in order to emphasize construction techniques. Once you understand the construction, any of the walks can be built in the more intricate patterns shown here.

Basket weave is the simplest of the patterns shown. By planning ahead you can lay the pattern and cut only a few or even no blocks at all. The secret is in making the walk an even multiple of the brick length, and in using a brick twice as long as it is wide.

Octagonal pavers are less intricate than they look. The paver is key-shape and designed so that two pavers will nest together to form somewhat of a square if you put one upside down next to the other.

Herringbone is a pattern that is simple to lay and keep track of, but expect to do a lot of cutting.

The diagonal herringbone pattern is exactly the same except that it is laid at a 45-degree angle to the edges of the walk. Consequently you can expect to do a substantial amount of cutting, most of it at an angle. The open field method, which is explained in "Laying a Paver Walk," beginning on page 70, eliminates much, but not all, of the cutting.

The patterns shown here have been laid in a sand bed but could also be laid in mortar. (For directions on laying these patterns, see pages 56–61.)

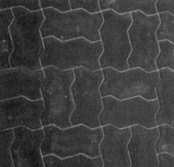

MULTIWEAVE BASKET WEAVE

OCTAGONAL PAVERS

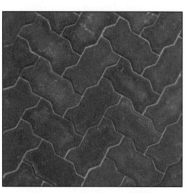

MULTIWEAVE BASKET WEAVE (ALTERNATE)

PAVER DIAGONAL HERRINGBONE

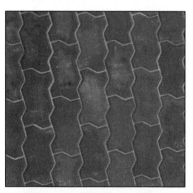

MULTIWEAVE RUNNING BOND

PAVER RUNNING BOND

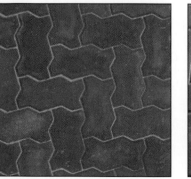

MULTIWEAVE HERRINGBONE

PAVER HERRINGBONE

7 SOFT-SET WALKWAYS

Soft-set installations refer to stone that is set on a base of compacted sand and gravel. The joints are filled with sand, which means that installation is easy for do-it-yourselfers. Soft-set walkways also offer a casual country look to gardens and backyards.

It's essential that excavation is level and that you create a solid foundation of compacted earth and a level sand base. Without a solid and level base, changes in weather conditions may eventually cause the stones in your walkway to shift, creating an uneven and potentially dangerous surface.

Because no mortar or concrete holds the path together, soft-set installations require a little more maintenance than hard-bed surfaces.

Laying a paver walk

REQUIRED SKILLS:
Laying out, digging, cutting, and laying pavers.

HOW LONG WILL IT TAKE?

Laying a 4×16-foot paver walk should take about:

Experienced .... 20 hrs.
Handy .... 24 hrs.
Novice .... 39 hrs.

STUFF YOU'LL NEED

✔ MATERIALS:
Gravel, bedding sand, joint sand, landscape fabric, interlocking pavers, edging

✔ TOOLS:
Spade, shovel, garden rake, rubber mallets, power tamper, hand tamper, level, broom, 3-pound sledgehammer, plywood-and-2×4 screed, paver splitter, wet saw or drysaw (also called a quicksaw), work gloves, safety glasses, dust mask

Concrete pavers require a fraction of the work that mortared walks require, yet they provide a solid surface underfoot. The walk is a system of materials: Landscape fabric lines the excavation that holds the walk, while compacted gravel placed on top of it provides drainage. A sand bed provides support, sand between the pavers keeps them from rocking, and edge restraints hold the pavers in place.

While paver walks share the same basic construction, many types of walks can be created. Pavers come in a variety of shapes, colors, and textures—and each can be laid in a variety of patterns. Edge restraints vary widely, too, from subsurface plastic to bricks to landscape timbers. With this variety the only way your walk will look like your neighbors' is if you happen to duplicate your neighbors' walk.

The success or failure of a paver walk depends largely on how well you compact the layers, including the subgrade. Loose dirt or loose gravel will cause sections of the walk to sink. Pavers need to be compacted firmly into the sand below them, forcing a bit of sand between the pavers and locking them in place. Compacting sand in the balance of the space locks all the elements in place. (Fortunately, you can do all the compacting with a machine.)

1 **LAY OUT THE PATH.** Lay out the path with batterboards and mason's line. Make sure the layout is square using the 3-4-5 method. (See page 38.) Check that your layout lines are level with either a water level or a line level.

Mark all the high spots with spray paint first, then remove them to level the bed.

2 **LAY OUT THE SLOPE.** Drive stakes at the corners of the walk and run level lines between them. To prevent flooding, the walk should slope away from the house at a rate of ⅛ to ¼ inch per foot. (Check local codes.) Measure down the appropriate amount on the stakes farthest from the house and slide the lines down to the marks.

SAFETY ALERT

Wear hearing protection, safety glasses, and a dust mask when operating a power tamper.

3 **EXCAVATE.** Remove the sod. Remove an amount of soil equal to the combined thickness of the gravel base, sand bed, and pavers. (The gravel base is 4 inches thick; the sand base is 1½ inches thick; the thickness of pavers varies.) Leave enough soil around the corner stakes so they stay firmly in the ground.

4 **CHECK THE SLOPE.** Measure down from the staked lines to make sure the excavation follows the recommended slope. The distance from the line to the bottom of the excavation should be constant and equal to the combined thickness of the gravel, sand, and pavers.

5 **CHECK THE BED.** Check the bottom of the excavation with an 8-foot straightedge to see if it's flat. Remove the high spots and fill in the low spots so the gap between the straightedge and the surface is never more than ⅜ inch. Compact the surface thoroughly with a power tamper running at full speed.

6 **LAY LANDSCAPE FABRIC.** Landscape fabric keeps the gravel from working into the subgrade and weakening the base. Spread a woven landscape fabric across the excavation and up the sides of the edges. (Woven fabric is the strongest.) If you need more than one length of fabric, overlap the pieces by 12 to 18 inches along the edges.

Laying a paver walk *(continued)*

7 **SPREAD AND COMPACT A GRAVEL BASE.** Spread a 2-inch layer of gravel across the excavation and rake it smooth. Compact with the power tamper running at full speed.

8 **BUILD A 4-INCH BASE.** Spread and compact another 2-inch layer of gravel. Add and compact gravel in small amounts until you have a base 4 inches thick. (If you were to put all 4 inches of gravel in at one time, the compactor would compact only the top, leaving the rest too loose.)

9 **TEST THE GRAVEL.** Make sure the gravel is compacted enough by testing it with a steel spike. If you can drive the spike into the gravel with anything less than a 3-pound sledgehammer, the gravel is not compacted enough. Compact until it is.

LAYING THE BED

1 **INSTALL EDGE RESTRAINTS.** Put in whatever edge restraints you have chosen, using the sloped lines as a guide. In this case the edging is a plastic restraint held in place by steel spikes driven into the compacted gravel. Use a restraint designed for pavers (not garden edging) and install it as recommended by the manufacturer.

2 **PUT DOWN BEDDING SAND.** Shovel bedding sand on top of the gravel to create a layer about 1½ inches thick. Rake it smooth.

The open field method

Simplify laying complicated patterns by initially putting restraints along only one side and the end of the walk. After you put in the sand bed, snap a line along it to show where the other end and edge of the walk will be. Lay the pattern, continuing each row until the pavers cross the chalk line. When you finish, you can cut the pavers in place with a drysaw (also called a quicksaw) and put in edge restraints.

③ MAKE A SCREED. A screed is a straightedge, usually a piece of wood, pulled along sand to smooth it. Ask a home center or lumberyard to cut a straight piece of ¾-inch plywood about 3 inches wide and as long as the walk is wide. Reinforce it by screwing a 2×4 to the back. Drive a nail in each end of the 2×4 so the distance between the nail and an edge of the plywood is the thickness of a paver.

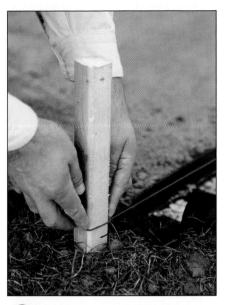

④ ADJUST THE SLOPED LINES. Slide the sloped lines down the stakes an equal distance until they are at the same level as the intended top of the sidewalk.

⑤ SCREED. Work with a helper to smooth the sand by guiding the nails along the top of the mason's line. Use the lines as a guide only and be careful not to move them by pushing down on them with the screed. Have a second helper add sand to the low spots and remove sand that builds up in front of the screed. Screed until the surface is smooth.

HOMER'S HINDSIGHT

ONE DAY AT A TIME
One of my more ambitious customers put in a long walk through his yard. The gravel was well-compacted and the sand screeded to perfection. The walk was a showpiece, but by its second summer it was at two slightly different levels. I was baffled by what happened until the customer mentioned that the day after he screeded, it rained and he had to wait to put in the last half of the pavers. Never screed more than you can lay in a day. If it rains on the unfinished portion, the extra moisture will keep the sand from compacting properly, and you'll end up with a walk on two different levels. If you have a bit of screeded sand left at the end of the day, cover it with a tarp.

⑥ SCREED A SECOND TIME. Starting at the end where you finished, work the other way across the walk.

Laying a paver walk *(continued)*

LAYING THE PAVERS

WALKWAYS

1 **STRETCH GUIDELINES.** It's easier than you think to get pavers a little bit out of line. Making a few little mistakes over the course of a long walk can result in a diagonal end rather than a square end. To prevent the problem stretch lines across the walk every 10 pavers and make sure the pavers align with them when you're laying.

2 **LAY THE FIRST PAVER.** This walk, which is a running-bond walk, begins by putting the first paver in a corner of the walk. Exactly where the first paver goes depends on the pattern you're using, but start against the house so that the pavers there are guaranteed to be full width.

3 **FINISH THE FIRST ROW.** Continue laying the first row until you come to the edge restraint on the opposite side. Cut a paver to fit in the opening. (See inset.)

A+ WORK SMARTER

CLICK IT

Many pavers have built-in spacer tabs for positioning. If your pavers don't, use the click-it method. Hold the paver by its top edges about an inch or so off the ground and bring it against its neighbor just hard enough to make a clicking sound but not hard enough to displace it. Drop the paver into place at the sound, and you'll get the proper spacing.

4 **BEGIN THE NEXT ROW.** In a running-bond pattern, the second row will begin with a half paver. Cut the block as needed to suit the pattern you're laying and put it in place.

5 **LAY THE SECOND ROW.** Continue laying the second row until you reach the edge restraint on the opposite side. If necessary cut the final paver to fit.

6 **CHECK THE ALIGNMENT OF THE PATTERN.** Lay pavers until you reach the first guideline. Check that the ends of the pavers align with the line. Make any necessary corrections before continuing.

7 **CONTINUE LAYING UNTIL YOU REACH THE END OF THE WALK.** Follow the pattern and work your way to the next guideline. Check that the pavers are properly aligned before moving on. Work your way to the end of the walk.

Cut the outline last

If you use the open field method, save cutting until you lay the entire walk. Then snap a chalk line along the intended edge of the walk and spray it with a clear lacquer to keep it from rubbing off while you work. Cut along the line with a drysaw, remove the scraps, and install the edging. Compacting the joint sand will rub off the lacquer and the chalk line.

8 **COMPACT THE SURFACE.** For stability the pavers must be compressed into the bedding sand. Compact the edges first, then the middle. Repeat, compacting in passes perpendicular to the first ones. Keep an eye out for pavers that crack during compacting. Mark them with a permanent marker to make finding them again easier. Remove and replace the damaged pieces and run the tamper over them.

9 **SPREAD AND SWEEP SAND ACROSS THE WALK.** Spread mason's sand across the pavers and sweep it into the spaces between them. The fine sand works its way easily between the pavers.

10 **COMPACT THE SAND.** Run the power tamper over the walk, first along the edges, then down the middle. Have a helper sweep sand to refill the joints, and compact again. Sweep and compact until the joints are full. Shovel soil into the edges of the excavation to cover the edging and plant the soil with grass or flowers.

Laying a brick walk

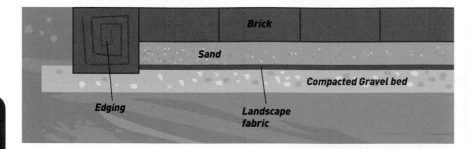

Brick

Sand

Compacted Gravel bed

Edging

Landscape fabric

Laying a brick walk is similar to laying a paver walk with the exception that the landscape fabric is laid between the stones and the sand.

Specs for sand and stone are the same for both brick and pavers.

Make sure to use brick pavers rated for outdoor use—SX if winter temperatures drop below freezing; MX in warmer climates—rather than building bricks.

Pavers come in a variety of sizes. When you plan your walk, go to the store, measure what's available, and design the width and length accordingly.

1 LAY A GRAVEL BED. Lay out and dig a bed 6 inches longer and wider than the walk in each direction and 5½ inches deep plus the thickness of a paver, sloping it ¼ inch per foot away from the nearest structure. Compact with a power tamper, then spread 2 inches of gravel. Compact the gravel until you need at least a 3-pound sledgehammer to drive a landscape spike through it.

2 INSTALL THE EDGING. Add and compact gravel until a 6×6 timber set on the bed is flush with the grade or no more than ⅜ inch above it. Drill holes for landscape spikes a few inches from the end of the 6×6 and every 4 feet in between. Spike the timber in place. Add and compact gravel to within 4 inches of the top of the timber. Cover the gravel with a layer of landscape fabric, overlapping joints 8 to 12 inches as necessary.

3 ADD AND SMOOTH SAND. Add enough sand so that the bricks will be level with the edging. Make a screed for smoothing and leveling the sand with a 2×4 and a piece of plywood that fits between the edging. Nail them together so that the plywood extends beyond the 2×4 by the thickness of a brick. Draw the screed back and forth until the sand is smooth.

4 LAY THE BRICKS. Lay bricks in the pattern of your choice. (See "Brick and Paver Patterns," page 55, for directions.) Stretch a guideline between two pavers to keep each line straight. Leave about ⅛ inch between bricks. Embed the bricks in the sand with a rubber mallet. Check for high or low spots with a 2×4 and add sand or tap bricks as necessary.

5 TAMP THE BRICKS. After all the bricks are laid, embed them in the sand with a power tamper. Sweep a layer of mason's sand over the walk with a broom or stiff brush to pack the joints between the bricks, then tamp again. Repeat until the sand completely fills the joints. Replace the soil around the edging.

Making a dry-laid stone walk

A dry-laid stone walk requires planning—and some muscle—to build. The walk is made of flat stones resting on a bed of sand and gravel. Dig a bed deep enough to accommodate 4 inches of gravel, 2 inches of sand, and the thickness of the stones. You'll invariably need to cut a few stones to make them fit. Aim for a gap of ½ inch between stones. After the stones are laid, sweep mason's sand between them to lock them in place.

Lifting stones is tiring work and can be rough on the back. Use your legs as much as possible when lifting the stones.

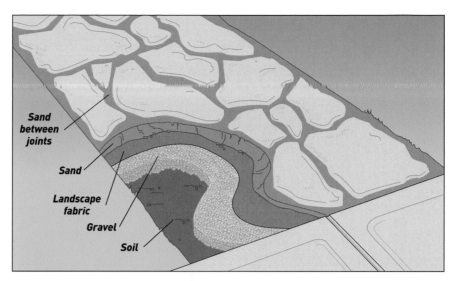

Sand between joints
Sand
Landscape fabric
Gravel
Soil

A STONE WALK ADDS A TOUCH OF THE COUNTRY TO ANY YARD. This particular walk does not require mortar. The first layer is made up of 4 inches of gravel that helps soak up water and provide drainage. Place landscape fabric for the second layer over the gravel to keep the sand from sifting down into it and to prevent weeds from growing through the sand. The third layer consists of 2 inches of sand that provides a compact yet firm foundation for the stones. The stones sit on top of the sand bed. Packing sand between the stones helps lock them in place. Using a variety of stone sizes makes the walk seem more natural, and they're easier to fit together.

SKILL SCALE

EASY | **MEDIUM** | HARD

REQUIRED SKILLS: Dry-laying stones is heavy work, but it involves only basic to intermediate masonry skills.

 HOW LONG WILL IT TAKE?

Setting stones to make a 4×16-foot dry-laid stone walk should take about:

Experienced . . . . 12 hrs.
Handy . . . . 14 hrs.
Novice . . . . 16 hrs.

STUFF YOU'LL NEED

✔ MATERIALS:

Stones, bedding sand, mason's sand, gravel, landscape fabric

✔ TOOLS:

Garden edger, mattock, spade, garden rake, 2×4, 3-pound sledgehammer, power tamper, rubber mallet, brick chisel, stiff brush or broom, garden hose, carpenter's pencil, work gloves, safety glasses, dust mask

1 **LAY OUT THE PATH.** Lay out the boundaries and slope of the walk using batterboards, stakes, and mason's line. Cut the sod along the edge of the walk with an edger and slip a spade under the sod. Press the handle down near the ground and remove the sod by kicking the back of the spade. Dig deeper, removing enough soil to accommodate a 6-inch base plus the thickness of an average stone.

Landscape fabric

2 **FILL THE BED WITH GRAVEL AND SAND.** Measure down from the mason's line to make sure the surface follows the intended slope of the walk. Fill the excavated area with 2 inches of gravel, then tamp with a power tamper. Add another 2 inches and tamp again until you have 4 inches of tamped gravel. Cover with landscape fabric. Spread 2 inches of bedding sand over the landscape fabric. If you need more than one piece of landscape fabric, overlap the sheets 12 to 18 inches.

Making a dry-laid stone walk *(continued)*

3 **MAKE A TRIAL LAYOUT.** Lay out the stones for the walk on the ground next to the excavation—this leaves the sand-and-gravel bed undisturbed while you cut and fit stones. A gap of ½ inch between stones is ideal. When you need to cut a stone, mark the cut with a carpenter's pencil, making the cut as straight as possible.

4 **MAKE CUTS WITH A BRICK CHISEL.** Put a brick chisel on the pencil line and strike it with a 3-pound sledgehammer. Score along the entire line this way. Then place the line directly above the edge of a piece of wood. Sever the piece with a single, solid blow.

Designer Tip

STEPPING OUT
Create a stepping-stone path by arranging the stones on the ground. Dig around each stone with a shovel or outline them with lime. Remove the stone, dig out the grass within the outline, and test-fit the stone in the opening. Add or remove soil until the stone sits at ground level. Sprinkle soil around the stones to fill any gaps.

5 **PUT THE STONES ON THE WALK.** Place the stones in position on the sand-and-gravel bed. Embed each one in the sand by tapping it with a rubber mallet until it is flush with the adjacent ground.

6 **CHECK FOR FLAT.** Stone walks are never perfectly flat, but check for high and low spots by placing a straight 2×4 across the length and width of the walk. Set a high stone with a tap of the mallet or by removing sand from beneath it. Add sand under the low stones.

7 **FILL BETWEEN THE STONES.** Once you've laid all the stones, sweep mason's sand into the joints with a stiff brush or broom. Since you can't use a power tamper on uneven surfaces such as natural stone, mist the surface with water. Continue adding sand and misting until the joints are filled to the level of the stones.

Laying a curved path

Laying out a curve

To lay out a radius, first lay out the end points of the curve. Put the end of a tape measure at each end point and stretch out the tapes so they cross at the same measurement. (The larger the number, the gentler the curve.) Drive a stake where the tapes meet and tie a string to it. Tie the opposite end of the string to a bottle of powdered chalk, and swing an arc. Let out more line to draw a parallel arc.

Lay out a free-form curve with garden hoses. Lay out a parallel curve with the help of sticks as long as the path is to be wide. Put a stick perpendicular to the curve every two or three feet. Stretch a second hose along the ends of the sticks. Outline the curve by sprinkling sand, lime, or flour along the hoses.

1 LAY THE PATTERN TO A STRAIGHT LINE. Snap a straight chalk line that connects the ends of the path, positioning it as near the middle of the walk as you can. If parts of the line fall outside the walk, snap a series of parallel lines until the entire length and width of the walk is lined. Lay the pattern beginning at the line and working out to the edges of the walk.

2 TRANSFER YOUR CURVED LAYOUT LINES TO THE TOP OF THE PATH. Repeat the layout process, marking the top of the path with a piece of chalk. Stand on the ground instead of the path when you draw the lines. Because no edge restraints are in place, stepping on the stones will displace them. Spray the chalk with clear lacquer so the dust from the saw doesn't erase it. Compacting sand into the joints will remove both chalk and lacquer.

3 CUT ALONG THE LAYOUT LINES. Cut along the lines with a drysaw. Cut along the entire line, cutting only as deep as the saw naturally cuts on its own. Continue cutting until the saw cuts completely through the material.

4 INSTALL EDGE RESTRAINTS. Put flexible edge restraints along each side of the walk, following the manufacturer's instructions. Complete the walk as you normally would, tamping and filling in between the bricks, stones, or pavers with sand.

A sidewalk is for getting from one place to another—a quick trip from the back door to the garage or from the street to the house. A rustic walkway, however, is about the journey, not the destination. Gentle curves that follow the contour of the landscape invite strollers to slow down and enjoy the view.

A rustic pathway can be as basic as a series of stepping-stones set at ground level. Consider spreading wood chips or gravel to define the boundaries of the path. Gravel can take on a slightly more formal tone when it's poured between two rows of bricks or pavers set on end.

Rustic walkways require little maintenance. In fact they grow more charming as they settle into the landscape, but occasionally you may need to add another layer of chips or gravel or pack some dirt underneath a stone to make the path smooth and level.

Making a gravel or wood chip walk

Gravel, wood chips, and bark are good choices for casual or lightly traveled walks—though you should expect to have to occasionally top off the surface with more material. At it's simplest, the walk is a layer of gravel or chips. More durable walks have brick, timber, or other edging to prevent the surface from spreading into the lawn. Flooding can be a problem and cause washing away with wood chips and bark, so pick a dry spot, dig out some soil, replace it with a layer of sand, and line it with landscape fabric to control weeds and to keep the surface level. Add a 4-inch layer of gravel or wood chips and tamp it for a firm surface.

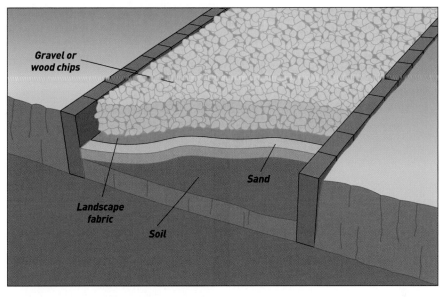

Gravel or wood chips

Sand

Landscape fabric

Soil

AT ITS SIMPLEST, A WALK IS GRAVEL OR MULCH SPREAD ON THE GROUND. The walk shown here is more durable. Edging keeps the surface from spreading into the yard. Sand provides a sturdy base that can easily be smoothed flat. If you want a mulch walk, bark mulch is less prone to rot and fungus. If you build a gravel walk, pea gravel and crushed stone make good walking surfaces. Check with your local landscape supplier. Some types of gravel and stone are available only in certain areas of the country.

SKILL SCALE

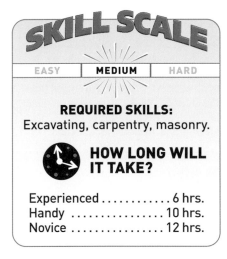

EASY	MEDIUM	HARD

REQUIRED SKILLS:
Excavating, carpentry, masonry.

HOW LONG WILL IT TAKE?

Experienced . . . . 6 hrs.
Handy . . . . 10 hrs.
Novice . . . . 12 hrs.

STUFF YOU'LL NEED

✔ **MATERIALS:**
Plastic edging, stakes, benderboard, 6×6 timber edging, paver bricks, concrete pavers, sand, landscape fabric, gravel or mulch, 12-inch spikes

✔ **TOOLS:**
Shovel, garden hose, garden rake, drum roller, hand tamper, electric drill, jigsaw, 3-pound sledgehammer, rubber mallet, wheelbarrow, safety glasses, work gloves

INSTALLING EDGING

PLASTIC EDGING is inexpensive and flexible and extends only ½ inch from the ground when installed. Dig a trench, place the edging in it, and align the edging with your layout line. Anchor the edging by driving stakes through the bottom edge with a 3-pound sledgehammer.

BENDERBOARD is thin pieces of wood—usually redwood—that you build up in layers to create a curve. Drive stakes along the inside edge of the curve and add layers of benderboard until the curve is as thick as the rest of the edging, then drive stakes to support the back. Screw them to the benderboard; remove the inside stakes. (For other curve options see page 87.)

Making a gravel or wood chip walk (continued)

INSTALLING EDGING

TIMBER EDGING—Lay pressure-treated or rot-resistant timbers along the edge of the walk and butt corners together. Secure the timbers by drilling holes for 12-inch spikes and then driving them through each corner.

BRICK EDGING—The best type of brick to use for edging is paver brick, placed on end or on edge. Dig a trench deep enough so the tops of the bricks are flush with the ground or up to 1 inch above grade. Place the bricks in the trench and pack soil around them.

PRECAST CONCRETE PAVER EDGING— Pavers also can be used in the same manner as brick edging. Lay the pavers flat or on edge in the trench and embed them in the ground with a rubber mallet until they are flush with the ground or up to 1 inch above grade. Pack soil around them.

PREPARING THE BED AND ADDING GRAVEL OR WOOD

1 **LAY OUT THE WALK.** Lay out the edges and ends of the walk with batterboards. Drive stakes and tie line to them to mark the finished height of the walk.

2 **DIG A TRENCH FOR THE EDGING** if the edging you're using requires one. Check that the surface that the edging sits on is parallel to the lines marking the finished height of the walk. If it is, the distance between the line and the surface will be the same along the entire length of the walk.

3 **PUT THE EDGING IN PLACE AND ADD SAND.** If the edging is set in a trench, pack soil around the edging to hold it in place. Fill the space between the edging for the path with a 2-inch layer of sand. Rake the sand smooth.

4 **SCREED THE SAND.** Flatten the surface by pulling a notched piece of plywood, called a screed, across the top of the edging. The depth of the notch should equal the thickness of the final surface, approximately 2 inches. Cut the notches with a jigsaw and screw a 2×4 to the plywood for strength before screeding.

5 **COMPACT THE SAND.** For a sturdy foundation compact the sand by moistening it with water.

HOMER'S HINDSIGHT

PICK THE RIGHT PATH

A buddy decided to build a walk out of wood chips with a lovely brick edging through his garden. What he didn't realize was the walk happened to be situated in a low-lying part of the yard where water accumulated regularly. Soon he had to buy another bag of wood chips to replace what the rains had washed away. When you build a walk, take the terrain into consideration and choose the right material for the situation. Gravel would have worked better for my friend.

WALKWAYS

Designer Tip

RUSTIC OPTIONS

You can make a decorative path by defining it with natural stones or pavers set directly on the surface.

Brick pavers and gravel or wood chips allow you to create an endless variety of patterns. If your edging is brick as well, the interior bricks can match or contrast with them.

Concrete pavers mixed with gravel or wood chips are easy to lay and create a pleasing contrast. Gravel or wood chips can be used between any shape concrete paver or precast block.

Making a gravel or wood chip walk

PREPARING THE BED AND ADDING GRAVEL OR WOOD *(continued)*

6 **PUT LANDSCAPE FABRIC OVER THE SAND** to help control weeds. Cut it to fit snugly against the edging. If you need more than one strip for the width or length, overlap the fabric edges 12 to 18 inches.

7 **POUR THE GRAVEL OR WOOD CHIPS** from a wheelbarrow onto the landscape fabric and spread with a rake. Take care not to dislodge the landscape fabric. Make sure the gravel or wood chips are spread evenly across the walk and against the edging.

8 **COMPACT THE GRAVEL OR WOOD CHIPS** by spraying lightly with water and rolling with a drum roller. Be careful not to loosen the edging by bumping it with the roller. Use a hand tamper for hard-to-reach areas or if a roller is not available.

LAYING A RUSTIC PATH

If drainage isn't a problem, you can build a path by laying a thick layer of gravel, bark, or wood chips directly on the ground. Even in well-drained areas, however, it's usually better to dig a trench and fill it with the path material. The sides of the trench keep the path from spreading out, working it's way into the soil, and eventually disappearing. Gravel lasts longer than bark or chips. If the choice is between bark or chips, bark will last longer.

1 **LAY OUT THE PATH.** Layout can be as easy as stretching out a garden hose to mark where you want the edge of the path. Sprinkle sand or lime along the hose to mark the ground and dig out a bed for the path that is 2 or 3 inches deep.

2 **SPREAD THE SURFACE.** Line the bed of the path with landscape fabric to keep the surface material from working its way into the soil. If you need more than one piece, overlap the fabric edges 12 to 18 inches. Spread the bark and rake it smooth, being careful not to poke holes in the landscape fabric.

⑨ HARD-BED PATHS

Hard-bed paths offer permanence, stability, and a more formal look than soft-bed styles. They also require more steps during installation. First you must excavate for the foundation, then you assemble forms, add rebar or wire for support, and pour, level, and cure the foundation. If your walkway is concrete, you're finished. If you're adding stone, brick, or pavers, you're only half finished.

After the stone is installed, the joints have to be mortared and struck. Then you might want to seal the surface so it will resist moisture and keep its color.

The payoff for all this hard work is a walkway that is beautiful, solid, and long-lasting. Your hard-bed walkway will remain secure through seasonal changes and weather conditions, weeds will not grow through the joints, and the surface will remain level for years to come.

Building a concrete walk

Building a concrete walk involves three projects: setting the forms, mixing and pouring the concrete, and finishing the concrete. The first requires using a hammer, the second requires muscle, and the third requires finesse. Consider building the frames yourself; ask friends to help you pour; and if this is your first concrete project, have someone with experience show you how to finish it.

The strength of the slab depends upon materials below the surface. A slab usually sits on a 4-inch gravel base that provides drainage. (In some parts of the country, soil conditions allow you to omit the gravel base. Check with local building officials to see what's needed.) A wire mesh running through the slab ties it together and helps prevent cracking when the ground shifts underneath.

The surface of the concrete has two kinds of joints. An expansion joint is a thick strip of resin-soaked felt put between the walk and existing structures so that they can expand, contract, and settle at their own rates. A control joint is a groove put in the wet concrete to form a weak spot: Any cracks that do form are likely to form along the weak spot, where they will be less obvious.

To mix concrete for a 4-foot-wide walk, 10 feet long, use about 10 cubic feet of concrete. A 90-pound bag yields about ⅔ cubic foot. You'll need at least 15 bags—nearly ¾ of a ton—and that's before you add water. It's more logical to call a supplier and have the concrete delivered ready-mixed and ready to pour.

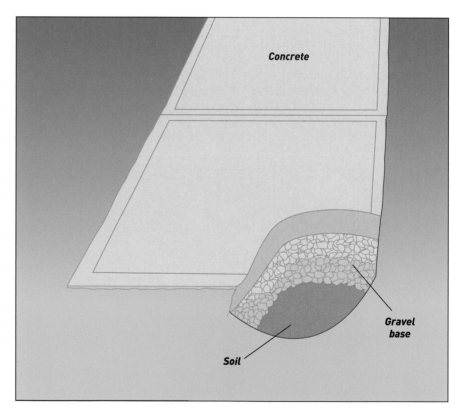

A CONCRETE WALKWAY IS A SYSTEM. Several components come together to create a concrete walkway. Gravel improves drainage and is easier to level than the earth underneath. Where the walk joins a solid structure, such as a house, an expansion joint allows each to move separately when the ground shifts. Wet concrete is held in place by forms and stakes, which are removed after the concrete has cured.

SETTING THE FORMS

Check for underground utilities before digging.

1 LAY OUT AND EXCAVATE THE WALK. Lay out the walk with batterboards and mason's line. Remove the sod and dig out 8 inches of soil across an area 1 foot larger than the pad in each direction. Compact the newly exposed surface with a power tamper.

2 ADD GRAVEL AND COMPACT AGAIN. In areas that require a gravel bed (most do; check your local codes), spread gravel on the surface in 2-inch layers. Compact each layer and continue adding gravel until the gravel bed is 4 inches thick.

3 LAY OUT THE OUTSIDE EDGE OF THE FORMS. Install a second set of layout lines on stakes. Position the stakes outside the first set of lines, offset from the first set by the thickness of the forms you'll use. Level the lines with a line level or water level.

Making curved forms

SHEET METAL: Round the corners of the temporary forms with 16-gauge (1/16-inch) sheet metal. Cut the metal about 6 inches longer than the curve and nail it to the insides of the forms. Shovel gravel behind the metal for support.

KERFED WOOD: Cut 1/2-inch-deep grooves in 4-inch-wide strips of 3/4-inch wood. Bend the board to follow your layout line. Drive stakes every foot along what will be the inside of the form. Then nail a stake on the outside of the form to further hold the curve. Before pouring remove the stakes from inside the form.

TEMPERED 1/4-INCH HARDBOARD: Cut the hardboard into strips and bend the board to follow your layout line. Drive stakes every 12 inches along the inside of the form. Build up the curve by adding strips of hardboard. Drive in a stake at the junction of the curved and straight pieces and nail together. Remove the inner stakes before you pour concrete.

Building a concrete walk

SETTING THE FORMS (continued)

4 **DRIVE STAKES ALONG THE NEW LAYOUT LINES.** Drive stakes along the layout lines, putting them at the corners of the walk and every 2 feet in between. Drive the stakes straight up and down and firmly embed them in the ground. You'll trim them to height later.

5 **MARK THE STAKES.** The walk must slope away from the house at a rate of ⅛ to ¼ inch per foot; check your local codes for the proper amount. Measure down from the batterboards and mark the corner stakes at the finished height of the walk. Hold a chalk line tight at the marks you made, and snap the chalk line to mark the rest of the stakes.

6 **NAIL THE FORMS IN PLACE.** Align a 2×4 with the marks on the stakes and nail it in place with two duplex nails. Brace the 2×4 with a 3-pound sledgehammer while you nail. Nail the rest of the stakes to the form the same way. Cut the stakes flush with or just below the top of the forms.

7 **PUT IN AN EXPANSION JOINT.** If the walk butts against existing concrete, place a ½×4-inch expansion joint between them to allow each structure to move separately if the ground shifts. Attach the expansion joint to the structure with masonry nails or construction adhesive. Brush a form-release agent on the inside of the form so it is easier to remove after the concrete has set.

8 **SPLICE BOARDS TOGETHER,** if necessary. On sides too long for a single board, butt two boards together. Cut a strip of ½-inch plywood and nail it across the joint. Drive a 2×4 stake at each end of the plywood strip and nail it to the form with duplex nails.

9 **LAY WIRE MESH** to help prevent the walk from cracking. Position the mesh in what will be the middle of the slab, using wire supports (sold separately). Mesh has a natural curve; set it so it curves down at the ends. If one piece of mesh isn't enough, splice two pieces by overlapping them 6 inches and securing them with tie wires. Don't let mesh touch the forms. Cut it to fit, if necessary.

MIXING AND POURING CONCRETE

Buy concrete in bagged mixes, concrete mixed from ingredients, or concrete ordered from a ready-mix company. The easiest method for small jobs—less than 1 cubic yard—is to buy premixed bags. All you have to do is add water. Mixing the concrete from ingredients—portland cement, sand, gravel, and water—is more labor intensive, but it saves money. You're not paying for the convenience of an all-in-one package. If you need more than a cubic yard, order the concrete from a ready-mix company. Remember, if you need only part of a yard, round up to the next full yard. If you need 2.4 cubic yards, for example, you'll have to order 3 cubic yards.

Cubic yards of concrete needed

AREA	SLAB THICKNESS			
	3"	4"	5"	6"
10 sq. ft.	.10	.14	.17	.20
25 sq. ft.	.25	.34	.42	.51
50 sq. ft.	.51	.68	.85	1.02
100 sq. ft.	1.02	1.36	1.70	2.04
200 sq. ft.	2.04	2.72	3.40	4.07
300 sq. ft.	3.06	4.07	5.09	6.11
400 sq. ft.	4.07	5.43	6.79	8.15

The chart above tells you how much concrete you'll need for some typical jobs. If your job isn't covered by the chart, some simple math will tell you what you need: Multiply the length of the proposed slab by its width (both measured in feet) to find the area in square feet. Multiply this amount by the desired depth or thickness of the concrete in feet. Then divide this figure by 27 (the number of cubic feet in a cubic yard) to find the volume in cubic yards. Add an extra 10 percent for subgrade variations and waste.

CLOSER LOOK

WHAT IS CEMENT?

Concrete is a mixture of sand, gravel, and cement. But what is cement? Cement is a naturally occurring stone that hardens when pulverized and mixed with water. The cement in your concrete, however, is most likely a manufactured product, called portland cement. The raw materials—limestone, cement rock, marl or oyster shells, shale, clay, and sand—are crushed, ground together, and sometimes mixed with water before being baked at 2,700 degrees F.

The resulting "clinker" is mixed, ground again, and mixed with gypsum. At long last the mixture is ready to be put in a bag and called cement. Portland cement is harder than natural cement, but both harden the same way. Adding water causes a chemical reaction in which water is consumed as the cement particles link together. As concrete comes up to full strength, it is said to "cure," something that continues long after the concrete has become hard enough to use.

BUYER'S GUIDE

CHOOSING CONCRETE

A variety of specialized concretes are available: vinyl concrete, fast-setting concrete, fiber-reinforced concrete, sand-mix concrete, and anchoring concrete. **Vinyl concrete** (or patching mix) is generally used for repairs. To make your own vinyl concrete, add a bonding agent to the mix of dry ingredients. **Fast-setting (or quick-setting) concrete** is made with Type III portland cement and dries faster than regular concrete. However, Type III cement is expensive and difficult to find. For a quick-setting concrete, use a ready-packaged mix with a quick-set additive instead. **Fiber-reinforced concrete** is expensive and normally not used by do-it-yourselfers. **Sand-mix concrete** has no gravel—only sand and portland cement. It is useful as a grout, but it will shrink more than regular concrete because it has no gravel. **Anchoring concrete** contains an epoxy cement that allows it to adhere to regular concrete and is 2½ times stronger than regular concrete.

Building a concrete walk

MIXING AND POURING CONCRETE (continued)

Concrete recipe

Portland Cement	Sand	Gravel	Water
1 part	2½ parts	2½ parts	½ part

The chart above is a basic concrete recipe to mix it yourself, with proportions of portland cement, sand, gravel, and water. The amount of water may vary—½ part is typical, but be sure to add only a little at a time. The maximum size of gravel you should use is ⅕ the size of the slab—¾-inch gravel for a 4-inch slab. Mixing is tough work. If you need a large amount of concrete, order ready-mix from a professional.

Mix the concrete as near to the work site as possible. The materials that go into concrete are heavy and awkward to transport and they're even heavier once the water is added. Clean out the old batch of unused concrete and rinse the tub or mixer thoroughly before you mix a fresh batch.

FOR SMALL BATCHES OF CONCRETE, fill a wheelbarrow no more than three-quarters full with premixed concrete or dry ingredients. Mound the ingredients and make a small crater in the center. Pour water into the crater a little at a time. Mix well with a mason's hoe or shovel, then test the consistency (see photo, below).

FOR LARGER AMOUNTS OF CONCRETE, rent a concrete mixer. Fill the mixer no more than half full with premixed concrete from bags, or add each dry ingredient separately. Turn on the mixer and mix the dry ingredients, then add the required amount of water from a bucket. Let the mixer rotate about 5 minutes, then test the consistency.

TO TEST THE CONSISTENCY, slice through the mixed concrete with a spade. The edges of the slices should hold straight and not crumble. If the edges crumble, your concrete is too dry and you should add water. If the edges fall over, the concrete is too wet and you should add more dry ingredients.

WORK SMARTER

READY-MIX?

If you decide to order concrete ready-mixed, make sure you're prepared to unload the concrete as quickly and efficiently as possible. The longer the truck is at your site, the more money you'll pay. This is the time to call a few friends to give you a hand. To help keep costs down, prepare the site as well as possible. Lay a pathway of 1×8 planks from where the truck will park to the site. Have all forms in place and secured.

Don't load up the wheelbarrow up to the top with fresh concrete. Not only will it be hard to move but the wheelbarrow will be very top heavy and more likely to tip over as you roll it to the site. Smaller batches are easier on your back and safer, too!

1 **MAKE A RAMP.** Rest a 2×8 or wider board on a concrete block so the wheelbarrow won't dislodge the forms. Also lay boards between the site and where the truck will park.

2 **PAINT THE FORMS WITH A RELEASE AGENT** such as vegetable oil. When the concrete is ready, carefully dump it in the farthest corner of the form. Place subsequent loads against the preceding load so the fresh concrete will mix seamlessly with what's already there.

3 **RELEASE TRAPPED AIR.** Once you've filled the forms with concrete, work it with a shovel, especially near the edges, to break up air pockets. Pull at the wire mesh with a rake until it settles in the middle of the slab. Tap the corners and edges of the forms with a hammer to help release trapped air.

Building a concrete walk

MIXING AND POURING CONCRETE *(continued)*

4 **LEVEL THE CONCRETE.** Use a straight 2×4 to level—or screed—the concrete. Move the screed in a sawing, back-and-forth motion across the walk. Make a second pass to finish leveling the concrete.

5 **FLOAT THE CONCRETE.** Slide a special trowel, called a darby, over the surface of the concrete. Move the tool in overlapping arcs, adding a slight sawing motion. Stop when a water sheen appears on the surface.

MAKE A SCARIFIER

If you will be laying a mortar bed over the concrete, scratch, or scarify, the surface so mortar will stick to it. Make a scarifier by driving 10d (3-inch) nails through a piece of 2×2. Drag the tool over the wet concrete in semicircles or arcs until the whole surface is covered with scratches.

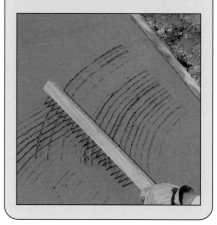

FINISHING CONCRETE

1 **ROUND THE EDGES.** When you've finished floating, separate the concrete from the forms by running the tip of a pointing trowel between the two. Slide an edger along each edge of the walk, lifting the leading edge of the tool to avoid marring the concrete. The edger rounds the edges to help prevent chipping.

2 **CUT CONTROL JOINTS.** Lay out shallow grooves for control joints, marking their locations on the forms. Space them 1½ times the width of the walk, or every 6 feet for a 4-foot-wide walk. Put the jointer at each mark. Then put a straight board long enough to span the forms next to the jointer and guide the jointer along the board.

3 **FLOAT THE SURFACE AGAIN.** Floating pushes down surface aggregate and brings a film of mortar to the top. Use a wood float for a rougher surface; use magnesium for ease. Float as before, raising the leading edge of the tool upward to avoid digging into the concrete. Stop when a water sheen appears on the surface. This can be the final surface of your walk.

92   HARD-BED PATHS

WALKWAYS

4 **BROOM THE SURFACE.** Brooming the concrete isn't required, but it creates a nonslip surface on walkways. Float the concrete first, then pull a dampened stiff-bristled broom across the surface, perpendicular to traffic flow. This creates small grooves that increase the grip on the walk. The longer you let the concrete dry without brooming, the finer the surface will be.

5 **LET THE CONCRETE CURE.** Cover the concrete with plastic to keep water in the concrete while it cures. Concrete that dries too quickly may crack. Let the concrete harden for at least five days before removing the plastic and forms. See "Curing Concrete," below, for more information.

6 **REMOVE THE FORMS.** Pull out the duplex nails with a hammer. Cover any imperfections on the sides of the forms with a slurry made of portland cement and water, then trowel with a steel trowel. Fill around the edges with soil and replace the sod put aside earlier.

CURING CONCRETE—OPTIONS

KEEP THE CONCRETE WET. Concrete dries by a chemical reaction called curing, which requires water. Let a slab dry out as it cures, and it's liable to crack. One way to keep it wet is with a sprinkler. Spray or sprinkle water whenever the concrete appears dry.

COVER THE SLAB WITH SHEET PLASTIC, which will trap evaporating moisture. If the final appearance of the slab is critical, staple the plastic to a frame of 1×2s. Otherwise the concrete will have a mottled look where the plastic touched it.

COVER THE SLAB WITH CLEAN BURLAP and keep the burlap wet with a hose or sprinkler for the duration of the curing. Adjust the water flow so the water doesn't puddle on the burlap. Turn the sprinkler on for a few minutes every few hours, as needed, to keep the burlap damp.

Tinting concrete

Concrete doesn't have to be gray. Two types of cement color products dye the concrete while you're mixing or finishing it, offering these and other colors: red, brown, buff, charcoal, and terra-cotta.

Liquid cement color, which is mixed on-site, is the easier of the two methods: Pour the liquid dye into the water in the mixer, then pour in the bags of concrete. This technique works best in small areas. Batches are limited by the size of the mixer, and the consistency from batch to batch is difficult to control.

Dry-shake colors consist of a powder that is applied to the surface after the concrete has been poured, screeded, and floated. Sprinkle on about two-thirds of what's required, work it into the concrete by floating, then sprinkle on the rest of the color and refloat. Work in small areas: If part of the concrete gets too dry before you can finish the three floatings required, the color will be splotchy and the top layer of concrete may peel off.

EASY	MEDIUM	HARD

REQUIRED SKILLS: Mixing, pouring, and finishing concrete.

 HOW LONG WILL IT TAKE?

Time required will depend on weather conditions, size of project, and level of experience

Experienced . . . . .Variable
Handy . . . . .Variable
Novice . . . . .Variable

STUFF YOU'LL NEED

✔ **MATERIALS:**

Liquid or dry shake-on cement color, expansion joints

✔ **TOOLS:**

Shovel, screed, edger, jointer, bull float or darby, wooden hand float, work gloves, safety glasses, dusk mask

SHAKING ON THE COLOR

① POUR, SCREED, AND FLOAT THE SURFACE. Pour the concrete into its forms, screed it flat, and float it until moisture forms on the surface.

② SHAKE ON SOME PIGMENT. Shake on about two-thirds of the pigment required for the area you'll be coloring. Cover the surface evenly so the color will be uniform.

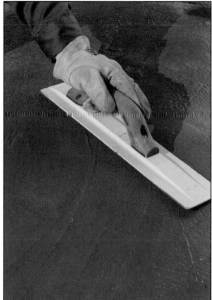

3 **FLOAT THE SURFACE A SECOND TIME.** Let the powder absorb the water on the surface of the concrete. When it has, float the surface thoroughly.

4 **SHAKE ON THE REST OF THE PIGMENT.** As soon as you are done floating, shake the rest of the pigment evenly over the surface.

5 **FLOAT AND FINISH THE SURFACE.** Float the surface again, mixing in the rest of the pigment. The resulting surface can be the final one, or you can broom the finish for more of a nonskid surface.

MIXING LIQUID PIGMENTS

1 **SOAK THE GROUND.** The night before you pour the concrete, thoroughly soak the area. Dry ground will pull water out of the concrete at uneven rates and cause streaking in the pigmented concrete.

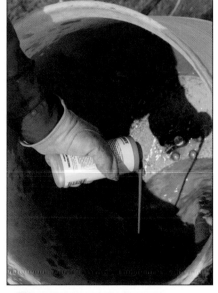

2 **POUR IN WATER AND DYE.** When mixing concrete with dye in a machine, the water goes in first to ensure that the dye is spread evenly through the mixture. Add the minimum amount of water recommended on the bag. (An 80-pound bag will need about 1½ quarts of water.) Once the water is in, pour in the liquid dye and mix.

3 **MIX IN THE CONCRETE.** With the machine still running, pour in the bags of concrete. If the concrete becomes too stiff to mix, add water until the mix becomes workable. Directions on the bag will tell you the maximum amount of water that the mix should have, but work your way up to that amount bit by bit. Pour, screed, and finish the concrete as you normally would.

Special surface finishes

Specialty surfaces offer variety from the well-known broomed surface. Stamped or tooled surfaces create the appearance of brick or stone. In areas not subject to freezing, a rock salt finish or an exposed aggregate finish creates a dressier slip-resistant surface.

A salt finish is easy to apply. Scatter salt on the surface, press it in with a roller, and wash out the salt after the concrete has cured.

An aggregate surface is one in which you cover the surface entirely with small stones. Although not difficult, applying an aggregate surface is time-consuming. Plan for it to take about three times as long as a broomed surface. Because of the time involved, you may want to break the walk into several small pours. Divide the forms into smaller sections with 2×4 dividers. Put expansion joints against one side of the dividers, pour one of the sections, and apply the finish. When you're done with the section, remove the divider but leave the expansion joint in place. Work your way along the walk one section at a time, always leaving an expansion joint between sections to help avoid cracking.

SKILL SCALE

EASY	MEDIUM	HARD

REQUIRED SKILLS:
Pouring and floating concrete.

HOW LONG WILL IT TAKE?

Time required for completion will depend on weather conditions, scale of project, and level of experience.

Experienced . . . . Variable
Handy . . . . Variable
Novice . . . . Variable

STUFF YOU'LL NEED

✔ **MATERIALS:**
Concrete, rock salt, aggregate, plastic sheeting

✔ **TOOLS:**
Concave jointer, concrete stamp, stiff nylon-bristle broom, floor roller, hose and nozzle, wooden hand float, bull float or darby, work gloves, safety glasses, knee pads

CREATING A STAMPED SURFACE

SCREED AND FLOAT THE SURFACE AS YOU NORMALLY WOULD. Stamp the surface with a commercially available plastic, metal, or rubber mold that creates a brick or stone pattern. Depending on the mold, it may be easier to stand on the mold to make the impression in the concrete. When using a mold that imitates brick, dye the concrete a brick color before stamping.

CREATING A PATTERN BY HAND

SCREED, FLOAT, AND THEN PULL A CONCAVE JOINTER ACROSS THE SURFACE, carving simulated irregular flagstone joints ½ to ¾ inch deep. When finished remove the concrete ridges along the joints by floating with a magnesium float.

MAKING A ROCK SALT SURFACE

1 **SCREED AND FLOAT THE SURFACE.** Finish the surface as you normally would: Screed it flush with the top of the forms and float with a darby or bull float until water forms on the surface.

2 **SCATTER SALT.** Scatter rock salt over the surface of the concrete at a rate of about 5 pounds per 100 square feet.

Don't make this surface in areas with freezing weather.

3 **ROLL THE SALT INTO THE SURFACE.** Push the salt into the surface of the concrete by rolling with a 90-pound floor roller. In a pinch you can roll the salt with a pipe or push it below the surface with a trowel. The floor roller will give you the best surface with the least amount of effort, however.

BUYER'S GUIDE

SALT OF THE EARTH

When salting a walk or patio, use water conditioner salt with ⅛- to ⅜-inch grains. Smaller grains produce little effect; larger grains produce a surface that is hard to walk on. While the average concentration is about 5 pounds of salt per 100 square feet, you can apply anywhere from 3 to 12 pounds of salt per 100 square feet for a varied effect. A light concentration of salt produces a surface that looks pockmarked. A heavier concentration creates larger, randomly shaped low-lying areas separated by smooth plateaus.

4 **LET THE SURFACE CURE.** Cover the surface with sheets of plastic and let it cure for five days. To avoid discoloration, keep the plastic flat and wrinkle-free on the surface of the concrete. (Don't use curing compounds or sprinkle the surface with water as it cures. Let the plastic do its job.)

5 **WASH AND BRUSH AWAY THE SALT.** Once the surface has cured, hose it with water and scrub with a stiff-bristle broom to remove the salt.

Special surface finishes *(continued)*

MAKING AN EXPOSED AGGREGATE SURFACE

WALKWAYS

1 **SCREED AND FLOAT THE SURFACE.** Prepare the surface as you normally would: Screed the surface flush with the top of the forms and smooth it with a darby (finishing trowel) or bull float until water appears on the surface.

Don't make this surface in areas with freezing weather.

2 **SPREAD THE AGGREGATE.** Spread gravel (which masons call aggregate) evenly over the surface of the wet concrete with a shovel and by hand. Cover the surface with a single, even layer of stone.

3 **EMBED THE AGGREGATE.** Push the gravel into the concrete with a wooden hand float, darby, or 90-pound floor roller. Once the aggregate is most of the way into the concrete, float the surface with a magnesium float, pushing the stone the rest of the way in. Keep floating until about 1/16 inch of concrete—but no more—is on top of the stones.

4 **BRUSH OFF THE CONCRETE.** Wait until the surface is hard enough to support your weight while you kneel on a board placed on it. If the board leaves an impression, wait longer. Brush the concrete off the top of the stones with a stiff nylon-bristle broom. If brushing dislodges the aggregate, let the concrete harden more before continuing.

5 **BRUSH AND FLUSH.** As soon as you finish brushing the surface, brush it again, this time washing off the concrete with a fine spray of water. You can use either the broom and a hose and nozzle or a special aggregate broom that you attach to the hose.

6 **REPEAT.** Let the slab harden a bit, then brush and flush again. Let it harden further, then repeat as often as necessary to get the desired surface.

Laying a mortared brick or stone walk

When you build a mortared walk, you build two surfaces—the one you see and the one that supports it and prevents surface cracks caused by freezing and thawing or rain. Build a support pad but place it 2 to 3 inches below grade. Lay a base of gravel—tamped well—for drainage and cover it with 4 inches of concrete. Don't bother finishing the concrete; leave the surface rough—mortar clings better to a rough surface.

SKILL SCALE

EASY	**MEDIUM**	HARD

REQUIRED SKILLS:
Basic to intermediate masonry skills.

HOW LONG WILL IT TAKE?

Laying a 4×16-foot mortared brick or stone walk should take about:

Experienced	12 hrs.
Handy	14 hrs.
Novice	16 hrs.

STUFF YOU'LL NEED

✔ **MATERIALS:**
Mortar, bricks, stones, expansion joint, plastic sheeting, 2×s, plywood spacers

✔ **TOOLS:**
Hammer, trowel, screed, rubber mallet, line level, mason's line, tape measure, level, circular saw with masonry blade, brick chisel, mortar bag, pointing trowel, jointer, 3-pound sledgehammer, paintbrush, carpenter's pencil, broom, cold chisel, pipe bender, work gloves, safety glasses, dust mask, knee pads

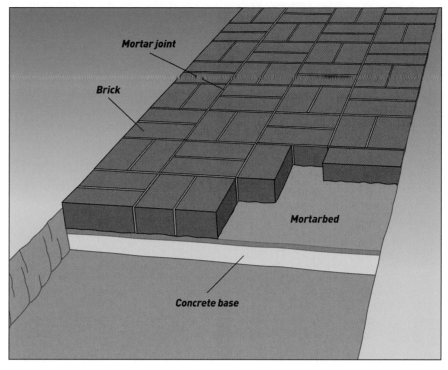

A MORTARED WALK BEGINS UNDERGROUND. A concrete base provides support and prevents surface cracking. A mortar bed on the concrete ½ inch thick for bricks and 1 inch thick for stones ties the concrete and brick or stones together and covers any irregularities in the surface of the concrete.

ASSEMBLING FORMS

1 **POUR OR PREPARE A SLAB.** The finished surface will sit on a concrete pad, which can be either an existing pad or one poured for the job. For either, the surface of the concrete must be below the finished grade by the thickness of the brick plus ½ inch—the thickness of the mortar bed.

2 **INSTALL FORMS TO HOLD THE MORTAR.** Set forms around an existing pad to extend ½ inch above the surface of the pad. If forms are already in place, as they would be on a new slab, build them up by nailing strips of ½-inch plywood to them.

Laying a mortared brick or stone walk

ASSEMBLING FORMS (continued)

3 **DRIVE STAKES.** To hold the forms in place, drive in stakes every 4 feet and nail them to the forms with duplex nails. Reinforce the corners by driving nails through stakes and forms.

4 **BUILD FORMS FOR ANY CURVES.** Make a series of cuts partway through a board to make it flexible. Butt the board against the cement base and drive in stakes every 12 inches to support it.

5 **PUT IN AN EXPANSION JOINT.** Put an expansion joint between the brick walk and any solid structure. Trim the material with a knife to the proper length and height and attach it with masonry nails or construction adhesive.

LAYING BRICK

1 **WET THE SURFACES.** The night before you start laying bricks, hose down the concrete pad and spray the bricks with water. Dry surfaces will suck the water out of the mortar too quickly. Let the bricks dry overnight and use only bricks that are dry to the touch.

2 **MIX MORTAR.** Empty a bag of type M mortar into a mixing tub or wheelbarrow. Make a small well in the center of the pile. Add a bit of water and mix it with a trowel. Keep adding water and mixing until the mortar is firm enough to cling to the trowel when the trowel is turned on its side.

3 **APPLY MORTAR.** Apply a ½-inch layer of mortar to a 2×2 section within the forms. If you work on larger sections, the mortar may dry out before you lay all the bricks.

4 SCREED THE MORTAR. Drag a straight 2×4 screed along the tops of the form boards to smooth and level the mortar bed. Fill any low spots with mortar and repeat.

5 LAY THE FIRST BRICKS. Lay a pair of bricks in a corner against the forms, separated by a plywood spacer of a suitable thickness: ½ inch for 7½-inch bricks, ⅜ inch for 7⅝-inch bricks. Tap the bricks with a rubber mallet to embed them in the mortar.

HOMER'S HINDSIGHT

SPACING OUT

When laying bricks in mortar, pay attention to the brick size. After my friend started laying his bricks, he realized that he had used the wrong size spacer to make the joints. Measure the length of the bricks first, then use a spacer that is thick enough to get you to an even 8 inches. Use a ½-inch spacer for bricks 7½ inches long, a ⅜-inch spacer for ones 7⅝ inches long. Otherwise you'll create a big mess set in mortar—like he did.

WALKWAYS

6 LAY GUIDELINES. Tie a mason's line to two bricks and position the line to mark the edge of the walk's first course. This is especially useful for long or wide walks, where it is easy to misalign the bricks. Lay the rest of the first course.

7 LAY THE SECOND COURSE. Lay the next row and those that follow it by setting pairs of bricks at right angles to those in the previous row. Separate the bricks with spacers and embed the bricks in the mortar with the rubber mallet.

8 CHECK YOUR PROGRESS. Once you have laid several courses, check your progress with a long, straight 2×4. If you find a low spot, put more mortar under the brick. To fix a high spot, tap the brick with the rubber mallet.

Laying a mortared brick or stone walk

LAYING BRICK *(continued)*

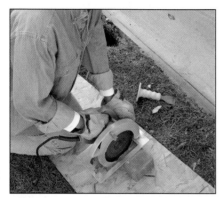

9 **CUT BRICKS TO SIZE.** If you need to cut a brick, score it with a circular saw equipped with a masonry blade. Place a brick chisel in the groove, then sever the brick in two with a solid blow to the brick from a 3-pound sledgehammer.

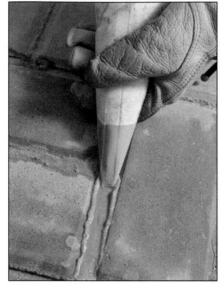

10 **PUT MORTAR BETWEEN THE BRICKS.** After the mortar sets, remove the spacers from between the bricks and fill the joints with mortar. To avoid spilling mortar on top of the bricks, fill a mortar bag with mortar and slowly squeeze it into the gaps.

11 **TOOL THE JOINTS.** Let the mortar harden until you can make an impression in it with your thumb without mortar sticking to it. Shape the joints by pulling a concave jointer along them.

12 **CLEAN AS YOU GO.** Don't let bits of mortar dry on the bricks. Remove the crumbs that come off while jointing by brushing with a medium stiff-bristle brush. Remove other mortar with either the brush or a piece of burlap. Sweeping with wet sand after the mortar has dried will sometimes remove bits of mortar that you missed. Cover the walk with plastic while the mortar sets. Remove the forms after two to three days.

Dry mortar

Dry mortar is a mixture of four parts sand and one part dry portland cement. It gives a walk a finished masonry look with less mess. Mix the ingredients in a wheelbarrow or mixing tub using no water. *Note:* Space the bricks with a suitable spacer: ½ inch thick for 7½-inch bricks, ⅜ inch thick for 7⅝-inch bricks.

Sweep the dry mortar into the joints with a stiff-bristle brush. Then sprinkle the walk with water. While the joints are still damp, strike them with a concave jointer. Cover the walk with a sheet of plastic. When the mortar hardens after a few hours, scrub the walk surface with a dry fiber brush to remove excess mortar.

WALKWAYS

A boardwalk is pleasant to walk on and to look at and is a practical pathway solution over terrain that doesn't lend itself to constructing a stone or concrete alternative.

Boardwalks run along the ground, supported by concrete blocks, or rise above the ground, anchored by concrete piers or posts, which means that excavating to create a level foundation is unnecessary. Boardwalks provide access to a beach or walkways over streams or marshy sections of land. Natural wood complements the surroundings and fits in with the landscape.

Building boardwalks is much like building decks. They are constructed of joists, beams, and flooring planks, along with posts and railings, to create a direct route from one point to another.

Building a boardwalk on grade

PROPERLY CONSTRUCTED, A BOARDWALK BLENDS INTO ITS ENVIRONMENT, becoming an addition to the surroundings rather than an intrusion. The walkway is restrained from shifting because it is securely mounted on concrete patio blocks and staked on either side.

Building a boardwalk along the ground requires little more than the materials involved and the ability to drive nails.

Use pressure-treated wood rated for ground contact; check that the label stamped on it reads "ground contact." If the drainage along the path of the walk is poor, excavate for a gravel base 4 to 6 inches wider than the walk and 2 to 4 inches deep.

The boards laid on the ground are called sleepers. If you want handrails on the walk—a good idea, but generally not required for a walk at ground level—make the sleepers from 4×4s. If you have no need for railings, the sleepers can be 2×4s. If the walk will be wider than 3 feet, put a sleeper down the middle as well as at each edge. If the walk will be wider than 6 feet, space sleepers every 3 feet on center.

For this project use a heavy 16-ounce hammer and 10d (3-inch) nails. You'll be driving lots of nails, and compared to a 12-ounce hammer, a heavy 16-ounce hammer will provide 33 percent more weight; the nails go in with a stroke or two instead of three or four. Multiply this by the number of nails you'll drive, and you'll appreciate the value of a heavier hammer.

Plan for less waste by using boards that are a multiple of the approximate width of the walk, then subtract approximately ⅛ inch for the width of the cut. If, for example, the walk will be 3 feet wide and you use 12-foot boards, cut each board about ⅛ inch shorter than 3 feet. Measure the length to space the outside edges of the walk.

1 **LAY OUT THE SIDES OF THE WALK.** Drive two batterboards at each end of the walk, spaced so the centers are roughly as far apart as the walk is to be wide. Tie mason's line to the batterboards to lay out the sides of the walk and check that they are parallel. If the walk will be wider than 3 feet, lay out a stretcher down the middle; on wider walks, space stretchers no more than 3 feet apart on center.

2 **LAY OUT THE ENDS OF THE WALK.** Lay out the ends of the walk with batterboards and mason's line. Check that the ends are square with the sides using the 3-4-5 triangle method (see page 38). Start at a corner and measure 3 feet along the end of the walk and 4 feet along the side. If the distance between the two points is 5 feet, the ends are square with the sides. If not, slide one line along a batterboard and recheck.

3 **IN POORLY DRAINED SOIL** dig a flat trench 4 inches deep for gravel. Lay out the trench by sprinkling chalk 2 to 3 inches outside the layout lines, then remove the lines but not the batterboards. Fill the trench with gravel and put landscape fabric over it to control weeds. Cover with sand, if desired.

4 **PUT SLEEPERS IN PLACE.** Put flat patio blocks along each side of the walk, spaced 4 feet apart and centered on the layout lines. Put the 4×4 sleepers on the blocks. Space the outside edges as far apart as the walk is wide and make sure that each 4×4 ends roughly in the middle of a block. Level the sleepers side to side and along their length with shims.

5 **STAKE THE SLEEPERS IN PLACE.** Drive 2×2 stakes on either side of each patio block. To prevent splitting, predrill a hole the diameter of the screw into the stake. Screw the stakes in place with 3-inch deck screws.

6 **APPLY DECKING.** Cut 2×6s to length and nail in place. Space the boards by putting a nail between them. If the walk has handrails, the decking must be flush with the outside edges of the sleepers. If the walk has no railings, the decking can overhang the sleepers by 1 or 2 inches. To make sure the decking boards stay parallel, use a framing square to align them.

Building a boardwalk on grade *(continued)*

7 **CUT POSTS TO LENGTH.** Handrail posts should be 35 to 38 inches high and spaced every 4 feet. Choose the height that is comfortable for you, add the combined thickness of the sleeper and decking, and cut all the posts to this length. Drill two ³⁄₈-inch bolt holes in the bottom of each post, spaced diagonally to prevent splitting. Drill the first 1 inch from the bottom and the second 2½ inches from the bottom.

8 **CHAMFER THE POSTS.** Set a power miter saw to cut a 45-degree angle. Cut a bevel on the top of each post to help rain run off the top. The larger the bevel, the more the runoff, but the exact size is up to you. Clamp a small board in place as a stop so that the chamfer is uniform on all posts.

9 **CUT NOTCHES.** Notching the bottom of the posts is optional but results in sturdier handrails. If you notch, measure the combined thickness of the sleeper and decking and lay out a line this far from the bottom of the post. Set your saw to cut 1½ to 1¾ inches deep and start cutting along the bottom of the post. Make repeated cuts, working your way up the post until the blade just touches the layout line. Knock out the waste with a screwdriver or putty knife.

10 **INSTALL THE POSTS.** Mark every four feet along the boardwalk and mark the center of each post. Have a helper align the center mark of the post with the mark on the rails of the walk. Then have the helper hold the post in place while you put a ⁵⁄₁₆-inch drill in the hole in the post. Drill into the sleeper and bolt the post in place. Repeat on the second hole. Install all the posts.

11 **ATTACH THE RAILING.** This boardwalk has three rails. Plan so that adjacent rails do not end on the same post. Clamp the top rail to the posts 1 inch from the top of the posts. Drill pilot holes slightly smaller than the diameter of a 2½-inch deck screw and drive screws through the railing to hold it in place. Once you have installed the top rail, install the bottom rail about 12 inches above the deck and the middle rail midway between the top and bottom rails.

12 **CLOSE OFF THE ENDS OF THE WALK.** Debris can collect under the walk if you leave the ends open. Cut a sleeper about 3 inches shorter than the inside distance between the sleepers supporting the walk to keep water from building up during storms. Tuck the new sleeper under the decking. Screw through the decking to hold the sleeper in place.

New sleeper

Building a boardwalk on posts

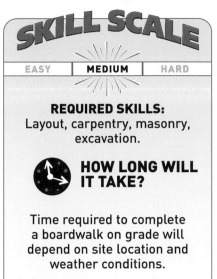

SKILL SCALE

EASY | **MEDIUM** | HARD

REQUIRED SKILLS:
Layout, carpentry, masonry, excavation.

HOW LONG WILL IT TAKE?

Time required to complete a boardwalk on grade will depend on site location and weather conditions.

Experienced . . . . Variable
Handy . . . . Variable
Novice . . . . Variable

STUFF YOU'LL NEED

✔ MATERIALS:

2×4s, 2×6s, 2×10s, 4×4 and 4×6 posts, wood preservative, flashing, ½-inch bolts, washers and nuts, self-drilling anchors, 10d (3-inch) common nails, 3d nails, 16d nails, 8d nail (1), form-release agent, ¾-inch gravel, bagged concrete, J-bolts with washers and nuts, angle brackets, joist hangers, post beam connectors, seismic/hurricane anchors, hanger nails, epoxy, ⅜×7-inch hex-head bolts, mason's line

✔ TOOLS:

Tape measure, chalk line, level, water level, tin snips, hammer, handsaw, circular saw, jigsaw, ⅜-inch drill and bits, ratchet and socket wrenches, hammer drill and self-drilling anchor attachment, plumb bob, posthole digger, shovel, mason's trowel, mason's hoe, wheelbarrow, work gloves, safety glasses, dust mask, combination square, framing square, stair gauges for framing square, speed square, 3-pound sledgehammer

WHETHER YOU CROSS UNLEVEL TERRAIN OR AVOID STONES THAT HURT YOUR FEET, a boardwalk is a great way to get from one spot to another. It's essentially a long, narrow deck. Posts extend from the ground to support beams, which run the width of the deck. The beams support joists, which run the length of the deck. The joists support the deck floor.

Building a boardwalk in most soils is no problem. The first question to ask is, "What's the ground like?" If the soil is inappropriate—or if the water table is high—build the walk on pilings. Pilings are long, heavy posts driven into the ground. Unfortunately, rental equipment will not do the job—you'll have to hire pile drivers to do the work. Check with your local building authority while you're in the planning stages to make sure the job you have in mind really is a do-it-yourself project.

Once you know that it is, think of the job as a long, narrow deck: posts sunk in the ground are set in concrete for strength, and crosspieces, joists, and decking complete the project.

Make sure local codes and zoning ordinances allow a raised boardwalk in your area before you start digging.

STANDARD SIZES

Because the width of a boardwalk is standard, so are the sizes of most of the framing materials. This boardwalk has 4×4 posts spaced 36 inches apart on center across the width of the walk, and 7 feet apart on center along the length. It has 2×6 joists, built-up 4×6 crosspieces, and 2×6 decking.

You can build a boardwalk up to 6 feet wide using the same size of materials. If you widen the walk, move the posts farther apart across the width but leave them the same distance apart along the length. If the walk will be more than 6 feet wide, consult a construction company.

Building a boardwalk on posts *(continued)*

LAYING OUT POSTS

1 **STRETCH LINES TO LAY OUT THE POSTS.** Stretch mason's lines parallel and 3 feet apart along the path of the boardwalk. Level the lines with a water level. Lay out separate lines on batterboards to mark each end of the boardwalk.

2 **LAY OUT THE POSTS.** Check that the lines along the ends of the walk are square with the first set of lines using the 3-4-5 triangle. From one corner measure 3 feet along the shorter layout line and 4 feet along the longer line. The corner is square if the distance between the two points is 5 feet. Apply tape on each line every 7 feet 5 inches for the support posts and mark the tape to show exactly where the points are.

3 **TRANSFER THE MEASUREMENTS TO THE GROUND.** Drop a plumb bob to the ground from the marks on the tape. Mark the spots with powdered chalk.

To prevent rot, a ledger must be pressure-treated redwood, cedar, or cypress.

ATTACHING A BOARDWALK TO A BUILDING

Depending on where you build your boardwalk, you may want to attach it to a structure—a house, a cottage, or an outbuilding. To do so, bolt a ledger to the structure.

If you attach the boardwalk to a structure, position the ledger so the top surface of the decking will be at least 2 inches below the interior floor level. This helps keep water from working its way into the structure.

Attach the ledger to the band joist inside the house with hex-head bolts or to studs behind the wall with lag screws. To fasten the ledger to masonry, you'll need to drill holes and install anchors to hold lag screws.

1 **REMOVE THE SIDING.** The ledger should be at least as long as the boardwalk is wide and the same width as the joists. Snap a chalk line to outline the ledger on the siding. Cut the opening with a circular saw, using a blade suitable for the siding and set to its thickness.

2 **REINFORCE THE FRAMING.** To prevent ledgers from failing, reinforce the attachment. Drive 16d nails through the sheathing, through the joist, and into the mudsill every 8 inches, driving the nails up through the joist and into the sill of the first floor.

WALKWAYS

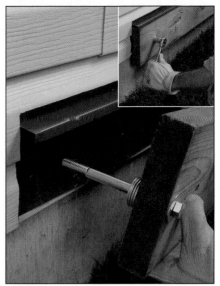

3 **INSTALL FLASHING.** Cut a piece of wide metal flashing to length. Tuck the flashing under the siding, leaving enough exposed to cover the cutout and extend over the siding below. Bend the bottom of the flashing to direct water away from the house.

4 **DRILL FOR BOLTS.** Level the ledger and prop it in place. Drill ½-inch-diameter bolt holes every 16 inches, alternating between the top and bottom of the ledger to avoid weakening the board. Drill through the ledger, sheathing, and band joist and out the other side.

5 **BOLT THE LEDGER IN PLACE.** Put a washer over the bolt and put the bolt through the ledger. Put on another four washers, then put the bolt through the band joist. Have a helper inside the house put a washer and nut over the bolt as it comes through. Tighten after all the bolts have been installed.

ATTACHING A LEDGER TO MASONRY

1 **DRILL THE LEDGER AND MARK THE HOUSE.** Drill holes in the ledger, spacing them 16 inches on center and alternating between the top and bottom of the ledger to avoid weakening it. Put a pencil through the holes and mark the wall to show their locations.

2 **DRIVE ANCHORS.** Remove the ledger from the wall. With a hammer drill and self-drilling anchor attachment, drive self-drilling anchors into the masonry until they're flush with the surface. Apply epoxy to the anchors to reinforce them.

3 **BOLT THE LEDGER TO THE WALL.** Put the ledger back on the wall, fastening it with the same combination of washers, bolt, and nut used to attach to framing (see Step 5, above).

Building a boardwalk on posts (continued)

DIGGING FOOTINGS

A boardwalk, like other structures, needs a foundation. In most cases you'll dig a hole for each post, put the post in it, and fill the hole with concrete. If you build along the shore, however, a high water table may require pilings instead of concrete and posts. If pilings are required, check with local building officials and hire a professional. When pilings are necessary, you can build the boardwalk around them using the basic techniques shown here. Consult a building engineer for span details and any change in joinery techniques to build the boardwalk on pilings.

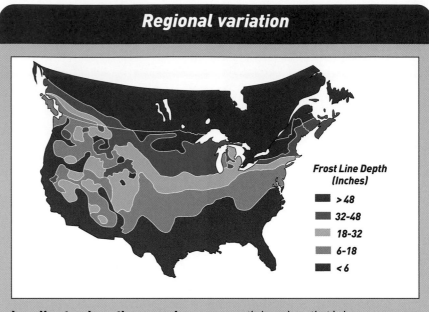

Regional variation

Frost Line Depth (Inches)

- ▪ > 48
- ▪ 32-48
- ▪ 18-32
- ▪ 6-18
- ▪ < 6

In a climate where the ground freezes, pour a footing so the bottom is at least 6 inches below the frost line. Check local building codes to find out exactly how deep that is in your area. In deep-frost areas, pour the footing and build a foundation wall on top of it once it's dry.

1 DIG HOLES FOR THE POSTS. Remove the layout lines after marking their locations on the batterboards. At the marks for the postholes, dig down 6 inches deeper than the frost line in your area. Make the holes about 12 inches wide at the top and 18 inches wide at the bottom.

2 ADD GRAVEL FOR DRAINAGE. If the soil drains poorly, dig 4 inches deeper, add 4 inches of gravel, and tamp well. Otherwise you can pour concrete directly onto undisturbed soil.

3 PUT THE POSTS IN THEIR HOLES. Retie the layout lines, then shift the tape marks 1¾ inches toward the end of the boardwalk, where they'll mark the outer faces of posts. Cut each post so it extends a bit longer than needed. Screw a 1×4 brace to the post.

4 **PLUMB THE POST.** Align the post with the tape and plumb it with a level. Drive a 2×2 stake into the ground and screw the brace to the stake. Plumb the post again while installing a second brace on its adjacent face.

5 **MIX SOME CONCRETE.** Empty a bag of premixed concrete into a wheelbarrow. Make a crater in the middle and add some water. Fold the ingredients together with a hoe, then slowly add more water. Mix and add water until the concrete is workable and clings to the edge of the hoe.

6 **POUR THE CONCRETE.** Shovel concrete into the hole around the post. Work a 2×4 in and out of the concrete to eliminate air pockets. Add enough concrete to fill the hole, then check again that the post is plumb.

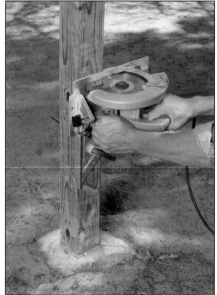

7 **SLOPE THE CONCRETE AWAY FROM THE POST.** Shape the concrete around the base so it slopes away from the post to improve runoff. Let the concrete set for at least 48 hours before removing the braces.

8 **LAY OUT THE HEIGHT OF THE POSTS.** Measure along one of the posts and mark the top. Use a water level to mark all the other posts at the same height. Then measure down by the width of the crosspiece—5½ inches. Use a square to mark this point on all four sides of each post.

9 **CUT OFF THE POSTS.** Set your circular saw to its maximum cutting depth. Rest the blade against the cutting line and draw a line along the bottom edge of the baseplate. Clamp a speed square to the post at the line and guide the baseplate along the square to cut into the post. Repeat on the opposite side to cut off the post. Cut all the posts to length.

INSTALLING CROSSPIECES AND JOISTS

With the posts set and cut to height, you now can put the crosspieces in place. The crosspieces sit directly on top of the posts and are attached with metal anchors.

The joists sit on top of the crosspieces and run at right angles to them. The easiest way to attach joists to the crosspieces is with seismic/hurricane anchors, also known as rafter ties. They're mandatory in earthquake and hurricane zones—and a good idea no matter where you live.

TIME SAVER

MAKE A STOCKPILE
If your site is a distance from where your materials are stored, it's wise to stockpile supplies close to where you're working. It'll save you trips back and forth for a few screws or an extra piece of lumber.

1 ATTACH THE CONNECTORS. Nail post beam connectors on top of the posts, bending the flanges so they fit snugly against the sides of the posts. Drill starter holes for the nails or hold a 3-pound sledgehammer behind the post while hammering to avoid loosening the post.

2 BUILD UP A CROSSPIECE. Make a crosspiece from two 2×s with ½-inch pressure-treated plywood spacers in between. Cut points at the top of the spacers to improve water runoff. Nail the spacers to one board, then place the other board on top and nail it in place.

3 INSTALL THE CROSSPIECE. Once the crosspiece is assembled, place it in the connectors so that the pointed end of the spacers faces up. Nail the crosspiece to the posts with nails designed for the connectors you are using.

4 INSTALL OUTSIDE JOISTS. The outside T-joists are flush with the end of the beam. Attach them to the beams with seismic/hurricane anchors. The boardwalk is likely to be longer than the length of a single joist. If so, cut the outside joists so that they end over the center of a beam and butt the next joist against the one you cut. Nail a 24-inch splice across the joint on the inside face of the joist, then nail the splice to the beam.

5 NAIL THE CENTER JOISTS IN PLACE. When you come to the end of a center joist, cut it so that it overhangs the crosspiece by at least 8 inches. Put the new joist next to it so that it overhangs the crosspiece by the same amount. Nail the joists together with 10d (3-inch) nails and anchor each side to the crosspiece with seismic/hurricane anchors.

WALKWAYS

LAYING DECKING

More than any other part of your boardwalk, the decking will determine its final appearance. This is where you might splurge a little. Pressure-treated wood is fine and durable for the understructure. While it's also fine and durable for the decking, you'll get a fancier look with cedar or redwood.

In order to have enough strength, the decking boards need to be 2×6s. They can be fastened with nails, screws, or decking clips. Nailing is the quickest and least expensive method. Screws are less likely to work loose over the years. Decking clips, which are nailed into the sides of the boards, leave the top surface with no visible fasteners; the best types attach on both sides of a board.

1 **BRACE THE CROSSPIECES.** Cut 45-degree angles on a 2×4 so that it's at least 2 feet long. Bolt one end to the side of a post and the other end to the crosspiece. Repeat for the other post supporting the crosspiece, bolting it to the other side of the post so that the braces won't run into each other. Brace every other set of posts.

2 **NAIL THE FIRST DECK BOARD IN PLACE.** Start at either end of the walk or at the ledger if there is one. Measure the distance across the walk and cut a deck board to this length. Nail it in place. Work your way along the boardwalk, nailing the boards in place and spacing them ⅛ inch apart. An 8d nail makes a handy ⅛-inch spacer. (If you're using pressure-treated boards, butt them together—they'll shrink ⅛ inch as they dry.)

Minimizing warp

Some people believe warping is reduced if a board is placed bark side up. But lumber companies and researchers have found that warping occurs no matter which side of a board faces up. So lay a board with the best-looking side up—unless you like tradition. To find a board's bark side, look for the high points in the contours of the growth rings at the end.

3 **SNAP GUIDELINES EVERY FEW FEET.** Snap chalk lines across joists every few feet, making sure the lines are parallel with the end of the walk. Measure between the boards and the lines as you work to make sure the boards are going in straight. Make minor adjustments to the spacing between boards to keep the proper alignment.

4 **ADJUST THE SPACING AS NECESSARY.** When you get within several feet of the end of the walk, lay out the remaining deck boards. If the last board is too wide or too narrow, adjust the spacing between boards to correct the problem.

Building a boardwalk on posts (continued)

BUILDING STAIRS

Most building codes require stairs for boardwalks more than 12 inches in height. To make them, here are a few terms: Stairs consist of treads and stringers. Treads are steps, which are supported by stringers—2×10s or 2×12s cut in a saw-toothed pattern. The rise of a stairway is the distance from the top of one step to the top of another. The run is the distance from the front to the back of the tread.

Treads typically are the same width as the boardwalk or even a few inches wider. Stringers should sit squarely on a concrete pad with the inside edges of the stringers at least 2 inches from the back of the pad. Designing stairs for your boardwalk may be the trickiest part of the project. Have a calculator handy and work through the formula provided below several times. When calculating how many steps you need, the boardwalk surface is considered a step: If your stringer has two treads, the stairway has three steps.

You can cut your own stringers, as shown, or if the height of your boardwalk is just right, you may be able to use precut stringers. Precut stringers come in 4- and 8-step lengths; you can cut them to make 2-, 3-, 4-, 5-, 6- and 7-step stringers. If you really want to avoid cutting your own stringers, buy precut ones, cut them to length, and then design the height of your boardwalk to match.

Because this staircase is wider than 3 feet, you'll need three stringers—one on each side and one down the middle. Do not leave out the center stringer, which may be a code violation. Leaving it out also will allow the steps to flex and wobble, causing a safety hazard.

Labels on photo: Riser, Tread, Stringer, Concrete base, Post

IN THIS PROJECT TREADS ARE NAILED DIRECTLY TO THE STRINGERS, which are cut in a saw-toothed pattern based on the rise and run of the steps. The stringers are attached to the boardwalk's face board with angle brackets and anchored to a post set in concrete. (For and alternative to this technique see "Building stairs with closed stringers" on page 117.)

Planning your stairs

	EXAMPLE DECK	YOUR DECK
1. Divide boardwalk height by 7 inches—typical rise between treads—to find approximate number of treads.	Approx. number of treads $\underline{\ \ 30"\ \ } \div 7"$ (boardwalk height) $= \underline{\ \ 4\frac{2}{7}\ \ }$	Approx. number of treads $\underline{\ \ \ \ \ \ \ \ } \div 7"$ (boardwalk height) $= \underline{\ \ \ \ \ \ \ \ }$
2. Round off to nearest whole number to find number of treads.	Actual number of treads Round off $\underline{\ \ 4\frac{2}{7}\ \ }$ $= \underline{\ \ 4\ \ }$	Actual number of treads Round off $\underline{\ \ \ \ \ \ }$ $= \underline{\ \ \ \ \ \ }$
3. Multiply number of treads by 11½ inches— tread width—to find total run of treads.	Total run of treads $\underline{\ \ 4\ \ } \times 11\frac{1}{2}"$ (number of treads) $= \underline{\ \ 46"\ \ }$	Total run of treads $\underline{\ \ \ \ \ } \times 11\frac{1}{2}"$ (number of treads) $= \underline{\ \ \ \ \ \ }$
4. Divide boardwalk height by number of steps— number of treads plus 1— to find actual rise	Actual rise between treads $\underline{\ \ 30"\ \ } \div \underline{\ \ 5\ \ }$ (boardwalk height) (treads + 1) $= \underline{\ \ 6"\ \ }$	Actual rise between treads $\underline{\ \ \ \ } \div \underline{\ \ \ \ }$ (boardwalk height) (treads + 1) $= \underline{\ \ \ \ \ \ }$

TO BUILD STAIRS YOU'LL HAVE TO CALCULATE: You'll need to know the number of treads, the rise between treads, and the total run of the steps—the horizontal distance between the top and bottom of the stairs. The chart above shows calculations for a boardwalk 30 inches high and provides space for you to write in the numbers for your deck. Once you have these figures and have double-checked them, follow the building directions.

1 **START AT THE BOTTOM OF THE STEPS.** Mark the rise on the narrow arm of a framing square by screwing a stair gauge to the arm at the length of the rise. Mark the run by screwing a gauge to the wide arm. Put the square against the edge of the board, as shown, and draw a line marking the bottom of the stringer. Extend the line all the way across the board.

2 **MOVE THE SQUARE UP THE STRINGER.** Slide the square along the edge of the stringer until the gauge on the wide arm meets the line you drew. Trace along the long arm to lay out the run. Trace along the narrow arm to lay out the rise.

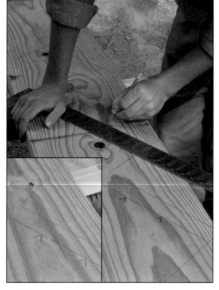

3 **MOVE THE SQUARE FARTHER UP THE STRINGER.** Slide the framing square until the gauge on the wide arm meets the line marking the rise of the first step. Trace along the square, outlining the rise and the run. Repeat the process for each step.

4 **LAY OUT THE TOP OF THE STRINGER.** Once you've drawn the line for the last rise, extend it across the stringer to mark the top end of the steps.

5 **DRAW A LINE PARALLEL TO EACH RUN.** The run lines you've drawn mark the top of each tread. Draw a new line to lay out the bottom of the tread—it will be 1½ inches below the existing line. This new line is the line you'll cut along. Mark it with arrowheads to avoid confusion later.

6 **DRAW A LINE PARALLEL TO THE BOTTOM OF THE STRINGER.** If you left the stringer alone, the rise of the first step would be equal to the rise you laid out plus the thickness of the first tread. To correct this you'll cut the thickness of a tread from the bottom of the stringer. Lay out the cut with your square, then mark it to avoid confusion when you cut along it later.

Building a boardwalk on posts

BUILDING STAIRS *(continued)*

WALKWAYS

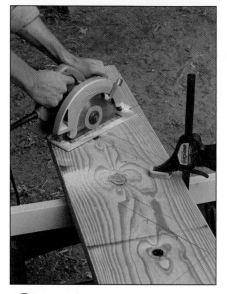

7 **CUT ALONG THE TOP OF THE STRINGER.** Set your circular saw to cut through the stringer. Cut along the layout line that marks the top of the stringer.

8 **CUT ALONG THE BOTTOM OF THE STRINGER.** Move to the other end of the stringer and cut along the line marking the bottom of the stringer.

9 **CUT OUT THE RISE.** Cut along the layout lines that mark the rise. Stop when the blade reaches the layout line for the tread. Repeat to cut out the treads, stopping when the saw cut reaches the layout line marking the rise.

10 **FINISH THE CUTS BY HAND.** Because of the shape of the blade, the saw will leave an uncut section of wood on the back of the stringer where the riser meets the tread. Finish the cut with a handsaw.

11 **MOUNT THE STRINGERS ON THE POSTS FOR THE RAILINGS.** Put the bottom of the stringers on grade, then dig a posthole the same size and depth as the holes for the posts that support the walk. Bolt a post to the stairs, as shown, then set it in concrete.

12 **NAIL THE TREADS IN PLACE.** Once the stringers are firmly attached, measure and cut 2×6s to length for the treads. Nail two 2×6s in place for each step.

If you build a boardwalk near a lake, environmental regulations may prohibit concrete pads because of the runoff problems they create.

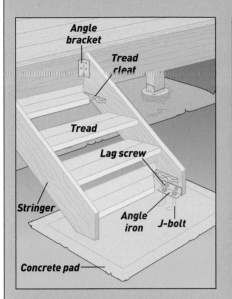

IN A STAIRCASE WITH CLOSED STRINGERS, treads are supported by cleats fastened to the face of the stringers and then to the boardwalk with screws and angle brackets. The base is anchored to a concrete pad using J-bolts, nuts and washers. Closed stringer staircases are easy to construct because they require less measuring and cutting than those with notched treads and risers.

1 **EXCAVATE FOR THE PAD.** Put the stringers against the edge of the deck to lay out a pad 12 inches wider than the stairs—6 inches on each side—and 30 inches from front to back. Excavate an area several inches larger than the pad for forms. Dig down 6 inches and level the base. Build a form and pour concrete into it, as described in "Building a Concrete Patio," beginning on page 142.

2 **EMBED J-BOLTS.** While the concrete is still wet, put J-bolts in the bed. They will hold the fasteners that hold the stairs in place. Position the bolts by having a helper hold the stringers in place, making sure the stringers are square with the joists. Cover the pad with plastic and let cure for 48 hours.

3 **REMOVE THE FORMS.** After curing, remove the forms, being careful not to chip the concrete. Fill in around the edges of the pad with soil.

4 **ATTACH THE TOP OF EACH STRINGER.** Nail one side of an angle bracket to the top of each stringer with 3d (1¼-inch) hanger nails. Put the stringers against the joists and drive nails through the other side of the brackets.

5 **ATTACH THE BASE OF EACH STRINGER.** Fasten an angle bracket to the base of each stringer with ⅜×1½-inch lag screws. Fasten the angle bracket to each J- bolt in the concrete with a washer and nut.

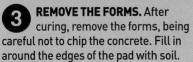

WALKWAYS

INSTALLING A RAILING

For safety's sake, boardwalks more than 30 inches high should have railings. Generally the required height for a railing is 36 inches, but check local building code restrictions on railing height and distances between balusters or rails—spacing should be less than 4 inches or greater than 6 inches so children won't get their heads stuck between them. Two basic options are available: a three-rail design topped with a cap rail or a two-rail variation with balusters.

Besides making a boardwalk safer, a railing adds a nice finishing touch. Topped off with a cap rail, there are few more convenient spots to rest your iced tea at the end of a hard day's work.

Railings add a finishing touch, but they are primarily functional, keeping family and friends from falling. Attach railings securely to prevent accidents.

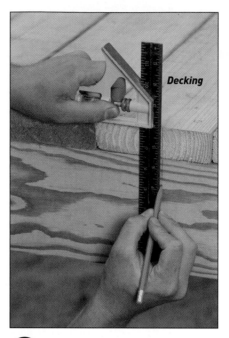

Decking

1 **LAY OUT THE POSTS** at least every 6 feet on center along the joists. If the walk starts at a building, place the first 4×4 railing post next to the wall of the structure and against the face of the stringer.

2 **CHAMFER THE POSTS.** Cut the railing posts to length. Mark a 45-degree bevel on the bottom outside edge of each post. Cut the bevels with a circular saw.

3 **DRILL FOR BOLTS.** Drill holes for the bolts that hold the posts in place. Position the holes so they will fall at least 2 inches from the top or bottom of the joist. To avoid weakening the posts, space the holes diagonally.

4 **BOLT THE POSTS IN PLACE.** With a helper, position each railing post so its bottom is flush with the bottom of the joist. Plumb the post and mark hole locations on the face board with the tip of a drill bit. Remove the post and drill ⅜-inch holes. Reposition the post and secure it with ⅜×7-inch hex-head bolts.

5 **INSTALL THE BOTTOM RAILS.** Cut 2×4 rails to length. Prop the lower rail in place on blocks and toenail the rail to the post with galvanized 10d (3-inch) nails. To make toenailing a little easier, drill a small starter hole for the nails.

WALKWAYS

6 **INSTALL THE TOP RAILS.** Place the top rail flush with the top of the posts and toenail it in place as you did the lower rail.

7 **INSTALL THE MIDDLE RAILS.** Toenail the center rail to the posts midway between the upper and lower rails.

Cutting away an overhang

If decking overhangs the edge of the boardwalk, it will get in the way when you try to attach the railing. Cut decking back with a saber saw. Mark the section you need to cut out and start at the end of the extending board. Cut toward the joist and turn the saw just before you reach it. Cut tight along the face of the joist and turn the saw around to clean out the corner, if necessary.

WALKWAYS

8 **INSTALL CAP RAILS.** Cut a 2×6 to length for the cap rail. If you need to join pieces, center the joint above a post. Place the cap rail on top of the post and upper rail, then nail it in place with galvanized 10d (3-inch) nails.

STAIR RAILINGS AND BALUSTRADES

INSTALL THE RAILINGS ON THE STAIRS. Put in the upper posts when you put in the railing posts for the rest of the walk. Bolt the lower railing posts to the outside edges of the stringers. The top of the lower posts and the ends of the side rails are cut at the same angle as the stringers. To determine the angle clamp a rail in place and trace along the posts for the angle.

IF YOU PREFER BALUSTERS TO A CENTER RAIL, install only the top, bottom, and cap rails. Position the balusters with a spacer—typically less than 4 inches or wider than 6 inches to keep kids and dogs from getting stuck. Space and nail the top and then do the bottom using galvanized 8d (2½-inch) finishing nails. Adjust spacing between the posts as necessary for a uniform fit.

PATIOS

Patios are additional living spaces that offer comfortable areas to relax with family and friends or to spend a quiet moment of reflection. A patio that is properly sited, well-constructed, and easily accessible is a pleasure to use and will provide years of enjoyment.

Although most patios are situated adjacent to the home, a gathering space located in a secluded area somewhere else on the property and connected with a compatible pathway is a pleasing alternative.

Three basic patio options are available: soft-set, hard-bed, and wooden structures similar to decks but detached from the house.

Your choice of materials will depend on the landscape, climate conditions, terrain, and the style you seek to achieve.

As you consider the design of your patio, think about how the space will be used most often. Is it a gathering place for family or a spot for frequent entertaining? If you entertain frequently, your patio should be large enough to accommodate a crowd and have plenty of comfortable seating and space for tables. Also consider devoting space for a grill or even an outdoor kitchen. The patio should be easily accessible from the house, especially the kitchen.

If your patio will be used primarily as a place to read a book or spend quiet time, consider a more intimate space, perhaps in a secluded place on the property.

In this section are chapters about soft-set and hard-bed patios, constructing connecting steps of brick, concrete, and timber, and instructions on building ramps to access raised spaces.

SECTION 3

REAL-WORLD SITUATIONS

WORKING SMART IS EASIER THAN NOT

Building a patio, even a small one, is a large project. Once the design is in place, the materials need to be chosen, purchased, and transported to the site. Here are some tips to help you get through the construction phase:

■ The project will probably take longer than you think, even if everything goes smoothly. It's outdoor work, and you're at the mercy of the weather. Working in the rain is no fun, and concrete needs to be poured within a prescribed temperature range to cure properly. Allot yourself reasonably long work periods. A full day's work on Saturday and Sunday will get you a lot further than an hour here and there.

■ Don't push yourself. These projects involve heavy lifting. Work slowly and take breaks as you need them. Consider wearing a back brace to support your back.

■ Wear the proper clothing and protective gear while you're working. Long-sleeved shirts and gloves are essential when handling concrete or cutting pressure-treated lumber. Also recommended for these tasks are a respirator, safety goggles, and a hat.

■ If you're using power tools with which you're unfamiliar, such as a masonry saw or a power auger, get instructions on safe use, and practice with the tool until you're comfortable.

■ Recruit a friend or hire some labor to help with the heaviest lifting.

■ Work methodically and review the overall project as you go to eliminate surprises and mistakes.

PATIOS TOOL KIT

3-POUND SLEDGEHAMMER

CIRCULAR SAW

DARBY

HAND TAMPER

PLUMB BOB

SHOVEL AND SPADE

BEAD BLASTER

COLD CHISEL

DRYSAW

HANDSAW

POWER TAMPER

SPONGE

BRICK CHISEL

CONCAVE JOINTER

DUST MASK

LEVELS

PUTTY KNIVES

STRAIGHTEDGE

BROOM

CONCRETE EDGER

FRAMING SQUARE

MATTOCK

RUBBER GLOVES

TROWELS

CAULK GUN

CONCRETE FLOAT

GARDEN RAKE

MIXING TUB

RUBBER MALLET

WET SAW

CHALK LINE

CONTROL JOINTER

GROUT BAG

PAINTBRUSH

SAFETY GLASSES

WORK GLOVES

PATIOS

Materials

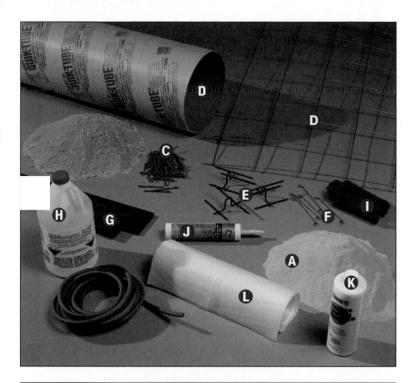

ⓐ Concrete comes in bag, or ready-mixed from a truck. Pour the concrete into either 2×4 or **ⓑ fibertube forms.** If you make the forms from 2×4s, use **ⓒ duplex nails,** which are relatively easy to remove. Before you pour, put in **ⓓ wire mesh** to help tie the pad together; support it on small **ⓔ wire support chairs,** and fasten it with **ⓕ tie wires.** Put a **ⓖ expansion joint** between the new concrete and existing concrete so the two can move independently if the ground shifts. If you're putting bricks, stone, or tile on top of an existing pad, wash it carefully with **ⓗ muriatic acid,** and fill the cracks and control joints with **ⓘ foam backer rods,** followed by **ⓙ caulk.** On brick, stone, and tile patios, brush on a **ⓚ bonding agent** to help the mortar stick to the concrete. Cover the patio with **ⓛ plastic sheeting** while the concrete dries.

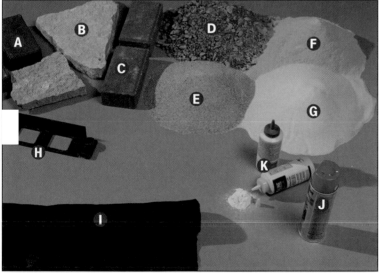

Paving materials such as **ⓐ bricks, ⓑ stones,** and **ⓒ concrete pavers,** can sit either on a bed of **ⓓ gravel** and **ⓔ bedding sand** or on **ⓕ mortar** supported by a concrete pad. On gravel and sand beds, a finer sand, called **ⓖ mason's sand,** is swept into the joints to keep the pavers from moving. **ⓗ Edge restraints** help lock the whole thing in place. **ⓘ Landscape fabric** is often used in a sand and gravel bed to keep the layers separate. Layout for a patio is done with mason's line and stakes or batterboards, but you can use **ⓙ spray paint** or **ⓚ powdered chalk** to transfer the lines to the ground.

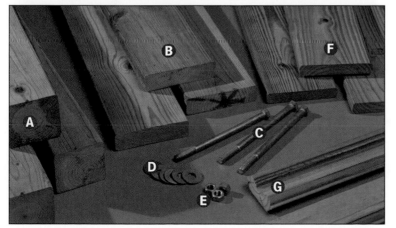

A wheelchair ramp is supported on **ⓐ 4×4 posts;** with **ⓑ 2×6 beams** and held together with **ⓒ ½"×8" bolts, ⓓ washers, and ⓔ nuts.** The surface is **ⓕ ⁵⁄₄ (five-quarter) decking.** Code also requires **ⓖ handrails.**

Soft-set patios can be made of natural stone, brick, concrete pavers, or tile. Built on a foundation of leveled and compacted sand, they offer easy installation and, if properly installed, minimal maintenance. With proper planning and organization, a soft-set patio can easily be installed over the course of a couple of weekends.

Brick and pavers can be laid in a variety of patterns. For variety add a border to enclose the design.

Because the stones are not bound together with mortar, edging needs to be installed around the perimeter to hold them tightly in place. Plastic edging held in place by driving spikes into the ground is available either as rigid for square installations or in flexible designs for free-form curves or circles.

An accurate layout is essential to a successful installation, so take your time to get it right.

Laying a paver patio

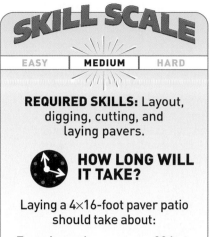
The design of patio pavers is a brilliant one. Even beginning do-it-yourselfers can master laying pavers without mastering the techniques of mixing and spreading concrete. And because no concrete is involved, you can start one day and finish another. Most pavers even simplify getting the proper spacing between blocks because tabs on the sides keep them the proper distance apart.

Here's how it works: The pavers lie on a 5½-inch bed of sand and gravel. The bottom 4 inches is gravel to provide drainage. The top 1½ inches is bedding sand that helps hold the pavers in place once they're compacted into it. Finer sand, sprinkled between the pavers, keeps them from shifting. Edging around the outside of the patio holds the pavers in place.

Because no system is foolproof, pay attention to details. When you lay out the patio, slope it away from the house at a rate of ⅛ to ¼ inch per foot to keep water from working its way into the house. Check local codes.

Make sure you compact the gravel in 2-inch layers. If you don't, the top will be hard but the surface beneath it will be soft. It will shift, creating ripples in your patio. Use the right sand in the right places and make sure the edging you use is designed for pavers, not gardens. Garden edging isn't strong enough. If you take more than a day to lay the patio, cover the bed with tarps between work times to retain consistent moisture content throughout the entire bed.

BECAUSE PAVERS ARE CAST THEY ARE UNIFORM IN SIZE, THICKNESS, AND COLOR. This uniformity makes them easier to install than brick, which can vary in size and shape. Paver patios are extremely durable and require very little maintenance.

Laying a paver patio *(continued)*

Paver patterns

Changing pavers, or the pattern you lay them in, can dramatically change the look of your patio without affecting the cost. The patio shown on the next few pages is an attractive, easy-to-lay pattern called running bond. It's pretty much the standard in patios and walks, but it's not your only choice, by far. Basket weave, shown here with a multiweave paver, is even simpler—if you plan ahead and make the patio a multiple of the brick length and width, you won't have to do any cutting. Using octagonal pavers gives you a more intricate look without making the job any more difficult than running bond. Herringbone, also shown in multiweave, will require about as much cutting as running bond but gives you an entirely different look. Diagonal herringbone is the most sophisticated pattern. If you lay it, make sure you have the patience to keep pavers properly aligned and are willing to do the extra cutting required. (For directions on laying these patterns, see pages 56–61.)

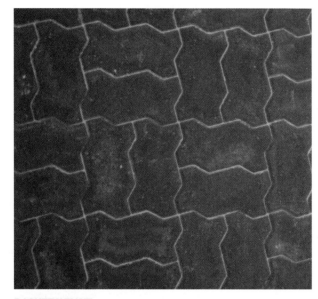

BASKET WEAVE

OCTAGONAL PAVERS

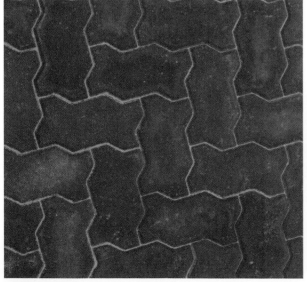

HERRINGBONE

DIAGONAL HERRINGBONE

LAYING OUT AND DIGGING A PATIO

1 **LAY OUT THE PATIO.** Lay out the outline of the patio with batterboards and mason's line. Check that your layout lines are level using either a water level or a line level, and drive the batterboards farther in as needed. For more on batterboards, see "Laying Out with Batterboards and Mason's Line," pages 34–36.

2 **SQUARE UP THE CORNERS.** Make sure the corners are square using the 3-4-5 triangle method: Mark a point 3 feet from the corner on one line and another point 4 feet from the corner on the other line. If the distance between the points is 5 feet, the corner is square. If not, make the necessary adjustments. Repeat for each corner.

3 **DOUBLE-CHECK FOR SQUARE.** Measure the diagonals of the patio. If the corners are square, the diagonals will be equal. If not, use a framing square to see which corner is out of square; correct it and repeat Step 2 and this step.

4 **LAY OUT THE SLOPE.** The patio needs to slope away from the house at a rate of $\frac{1}{8}$ to $\frac{1}{4}$ inch per foot to prevent flooding. Check what's required locally. To lay out the slope, first drive stakes about 1 foot beyond the corners of the patio. Run level lines between them with the help of either a line level or a water level. Measure down the appropriate amount on the stakes farthest from the house. Slide the lines down to the marks.

5 **LAY OUT A GRID.** Drive stakes every 4 feet approximately 1 foot outside the layout lines. Tie mason's line to the stakes to lay out a grid that follows the slope of the lines laid out in Step 4.

6 **EXCAVATE.** The highest point of a patio surface can be as much as an inch above grade—enough so that the lowest section is at grade. Remove the sod. Then remove $4\frac{1}{2}$ inches of soil plus the thickness of the pavers to make room for a 4-inch gravel bed and a $1\frac{1}{2}$-inch sand base, leaving the lowest surface of the pavers 1 inch above grade. Excavate the rest of the patio, following the slope of the lines.

Laying a paver patio

LAYING OUT AND DIGGING A PATIO *(continued)*

7 **CHECK THE SLOPE.** Measure down from the staked lines to make sure the excavation follows the slope. If the slope is correct, the distance from the line to the bottom of the excavation will be constant. Dig or add soil to correct any problems.

Wear ear protection, safety glasses, and a dust mask when operating a power tamper.

8 **CHECK THE BED** using an 8-foot straightedge or have a home center cut an 8-foot length of plywood, 3 to 6 inches wide, that you can use as a straightedge. Check the bottom of the excavation with it to see whether it's flat. Mark high spots with spray paint. Remove them and use the soil to fill in low spots so that the gap between the straightedge and the surface is never more than ⅜ inch. Compact the surface with a power tamper running at full speed.

9 **PUT DOWN LANDSCAPE FABRIC.** Landscape fabric keeps gravel from working into the subgrade and weakening the base—woven fabric is best. Spread the landscape fabric across the excavation and up the sides. If you need more than one length of fabric, overlap the edges by 12 to 18 inches.

10 **SPREAD AND COMPACT A GRAVEL BASE** in layers. If you were to put in all 4 inches of gravel at one time, the power tamper would compact only the top, leaving the rest too loose. Spread a 2-inch layer of gravel across the excavation and rake it smooth. Compact with the power tamper running at full speed.

11 **BUILD A 4-INCH BASE.** Spread and compact another 2-inch layer of gravel. Once compacted, the layers won't be quite 4 inches deep, so add and compact gravel in small amounts until you have a 4-inch-thick base.

12 **TEST THE GRAVEL.** Test the compaction of the gravel by driving a landscape spike into it with a 3-pound sledgehammer. If the gravel holds firm, the base is compact. If you can use less than a 3-pound sledgehammer to drive in the spike, compact again.

128 SOFT-SET PATIOS

INSTALLING EDGING AND LAYING THE SAND

1 **INSTALL EDGING.** Use a structure as the edge restraint for one side of the patio. Put edging along one of the adjoining sides. (You'll put in the rest of the edging after the pavers are installed.) Use the layout lines as a guide for both the proper location and slope of the pavers. Make sure you use an edging designed for pavers rather than garden edging, and follow the manufacturer's directions. In this example the edging is a plastic restraint held in place by landscape spikes driven into the compacted gravel.

2 **PUT DOWN BEDDING SAND.** Shovel bedding sand on top of the gravel to create a layer about 1½ inches deep. Rake the bedding sand smooth.

Any time you pick up a shovel, you risk straining your back. If you haven't been digging ditches for the last five years, ease into the job.

3 **MAKE A SCREED.** A screed is a straightedge, usually a piece of wood, that you pull along the sand to smooth it. Have a home center or lumberyard cut a straight piece of ¾-inch plywood 8 feet long and about 3 inches wide. Reinforce it by screwing a 2×4 to the back. Drive a nail in each end of the 2×4 so the distance between the nail and an edge of the plywood is the thickness of a paver.

4 **ADJUST THE SLOPED LINES.** Remove all the lines perpendicular to the slope except the one at the edge. Remove every second sloped line so there are lines at the edges of the patio and every 8 feet in between. Slide the sloped lines down the stakes. Move each line an equal distance until it is at the same level as the intended top of the patio.

5 **SCREED.** Work with a helper to smooth the sand by guiding the nails along the top of the mason's lines. Use the lines as a guide only and be careful not to move them by pushing down on them with the screed. Have a second helper add sand to the low spots and remove sand that builds up behind the screed. Repeat until the surface is smooth. After you screed the sand, screed it again, starting at the end where you finished and working in the opposite direction across the patio.

Laying a paver patio *(continued)*

LAYING THE PAVERS

1 **STRETCH GUIDELINES.** Lay a sample row of pavers on each side of the patio and stretch lines to mark the ends of the rows. Remove the pavers and use the lines as a reference while laying the pavers to make sure you are laying them in straight lines.

2 **LAY THE FIRST PAVER.** This patio, which is a running bond pattern, begins by putting the first paver in a corner of the patio. Exactly where the first paver goes depends on the pattern you use. (See pages 56–61 for more information.)

3 **LAY THE SECOND PAVER.** Cut a paver in half and put it next to the first one. Depending on the pattern, you may be able to cut pavers in place or wait until the end and cut most of the partial pavers at once. The running bond pattern requires a half paver. Cut it with a wet saw, drysaw (also called a quicksaw), or paver splitter.

SAFETY ALERT

Wear ear protection, safety glasses, and a dust mask when cutting pavers.

A+ WORK SMARTER

CLICK IT
Many pavers have built-in spacer tabs for positioning. If yours don't, use the click-it method. Hold the paver by its top edges about an inch or so off the ground and bring it against its neighbor just hard enough to make a clicking sound but not hard enough to displace it. Drop the paver into place at the sound, and you'll get the proper spacing.

4 **FINISH LAYING THE FIRST ROW.** Lay the rest of the row, alternating full pavers and half pavers for running bond. (To lay other patterns, see the directions on pages 56–61.)

5 **LAY THE SECOND ROW.** Lay the row according to the pattern you're using. For running bond, this row and all but the last row are composed of full pavers.

PATIOS

6 **CHECK THE PATTERN ALIGNMENT.**
Lay pavers, checking them against the staked lines as you go. Periodically stretch a line, as shown, to check that the ends of the pavers align. Make corrections as necessary while laying the pavers.

7 **CONTINUE LAYING PAST THE EDGES OF THE PATIO.** Continue laying pavers as called for by the pattern to the edges of the patio. If a brick is too long, lay it anyway and save your cutting until you've laid the entire patio.

8 **CUT THE PAVERS ON THE GROUND.**
Snap a chalk line where the edge of the patio should be and spray it with a clear lacquer to keep it from rubbing off while you work. Cut along the line with a drysaw and remove the scraps. Compacting the joint sand will rub off the lacquer and the chalk line.

9 **INSTALL THE EDGING.** Put edging along the side of the patio you just cut and along the bottom edge of the patio. Drive landscape spikes through the holes to fasten plastic edging. If you use 4×4s, drill holes for the spikes first. If you use 2×4s, put them in place, drive stakes behind them, and nail the stakes to them.

10 **COMPACT THE SURFACE.** For stability the pavers must be compressed into the bedding sand. Compact the edges first, then the middle. Repeat, compacting in passes perpendicular to the first ones. Keep an eye out for pavers that crack during compacting. As you work, mark any cracked pavers with a permanent marker to make finding them again easier. Remove and replace the damaged pieces and run the power tamper over them.

11 **SPREAD AND SWEEP SAND ACROSS THE PATIO.** Spread mason's sand across the pavers and sweep it into the spaces between them. Mason's sand is fine and works its way easily into the cracks.

Run the power tamper over the patio, first along the edges, then down the middle. Have a helper sweep sand to refill the joints, and compact again. Keep sweeping and compacting until the joints are full. Shovel soil into the edges of the excavation to cover the edging, and plant the soil with grass or flowers.

Laying bricks on a sand-and-gravel base

A base of sand over gravel supports concrete bricks as well as it supports concrete pavers. The bed for brick, however, is slightly different: The landscape fabric goes over the stone rather than under it.

Use a paver brick (as opposed to a building brick) that is rated for outdoor use. Use SW brick in areas that freeze and MW brick in areas that don't.

Paver bricks come in various sizes. Each is smaller than its given size by the thickness of a mortar joint. Measure the paver you intend to use and design the length and width of your patio accordingly.

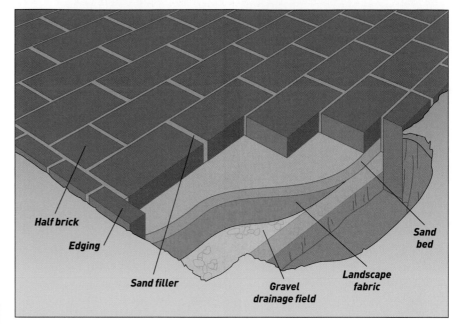

A BRICK PATIO BEGINS WITH A 4-INCH LAYER OF STONES, which provide drainage. A layer of sand provides a smooth bed for the bricks. Make sure you use a paver brick rated for outdoor use. Fill joints between bricks with sand to help lock them in place.

Labels on diagram: Half brick • Edging • Sand filler • Gravel drainage field • Landscape fabric • Sand bed

SKILL SCALE

EASY	**MEDIUM**	HARD

REQUIRED SKILLS:
Basic masonry skills.

HOW LONG WILL IT TAKE?

Laying an 8×10-foot patio of bricks will take about:

Experienced	8 hrs.
Handy	10 hrs.
Novice	12 hrs.

STUFF YOU'LL NEED

✔ MATERIALS:
Bricks, bedding and mason's sand, gravel, landscape spikes, landscape fabric, edging

✔ TOOLS:
Mason's line, rubber mallet, framing square, level, 3-pound sledgehammer, brick chisel, brush or broom, power tamper, garden hose, safety glasses, work gloves, knee pads, dust mask, ear protection

LAY BRICKS

1 LAY A GRAVEL BED. Lay out and dig a bed that is 5½ inches deep plus the thickness of a brick, sloping the bed ¼ inch per foot away from the house. Compact the soil with a power tamper. Spread a 2-inch layer of gravel, and compact. Add and compact gravel in 2-inch layers or less until the bed is 4 inches deep. The bed is firm enough when you can't drive a spike into it with anything less than a 3-pound sledgehammer.

2 INSTALL LANDSCAPE FABRIC, A SAND BED, AND EDGING. Spread a layer of landscape fabric on the gravel to keep the sand from filtering into the gravel. Overlap rows of fabric by 12 to 18 inches. Install edging, anchoring it as directed by the manufacturer. Spread a 1½-inch-thick layer of sand and flatten it with a screed (see page 129, Step 15).

3 **LAY A BORDER.** The finished walk will look best if you lay a row of bricks around the edges. Lay the bricks lengthwise against the edging. Plan so you won't have to trim any bricks to width while laying the final row.

Wear safety glasses and a dust mask when cutting bricks.

4 **LAY THE FIRST ROW.** Start laying the bricks from one corner, spacing them ⅛ inch apart or less. On a large patio, run a mason's line across the patio to mark the edge of the bricks.

5 **BED THE BRICKS.** Use a rubber mallet to tap the bricks into place on the sand bed. Use a level to make sure the bricks are the same height as the edging. If a brick is too high, remove some sand from under it. If a brick is too low, use extra sand to fill the depression.

6 **CONTINUE LAYING THE PATTERN.** On the running bond pattern used here, the first brick of every other row is a half brick. Lay out the cut for the half brick and cut several in advance so you can work without pausing to cut. Lay them as you go. Herringbone and other patterns require even more cutting. (For more details about cutting brick, see pages 56–61.)

7 **CHECK FOR FLAT.** As you lay rows, keep checking the patio surface for high and low spots by putting a straight 2×4 or a level across the bricks. Seat high spots with a tap from the rubber mallet. Add sand to shore up low spots. Continue laying bricks as described in Steps 4–6.

8 **SEAT THE BRICKS.** Pass over the patio with a power tamper. Then pour fine sand—sold as mason's sand—across the patio and sweep it into the joints between bricks. Tamp, sweep more sand, and repeat until all joints are filled.

Laying a curved edge

Even though bricks and pavers are rectangular and tape measures are straight, walks and patios can have curves and angles.

After you've laid a patio or walkway, you can use a handheld portable masonry saw (also known as a drysaw) to shape the edges.

Before laying the patio, lay out the curve on the ground using one of the techniques described on page 135.

Lay the patio as you normally would, laying the bricks right up to or just past the layout line. Cut the edge to shape and install the edge restraints as the final step.

CURVED EDGES BREAK UP THE SQUARE LINES OF A PATIO AND ADD A LITTLE DRAMA TO A GEOMETRICAL LAYOUT. Curves can follow a prescribed arc, as shown here, or undulate in a more free-form manner.

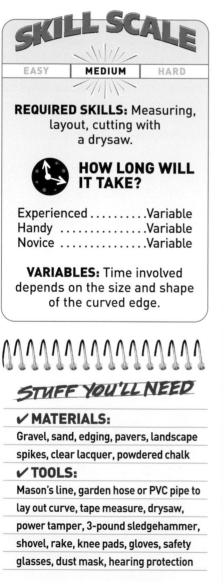

SKILL SCALE

EASY | **MEDIUM** | HARD

REQUIRED SKILLS: Measuring, layout, cutting with a drysaw.

HOW LONG WILL IT TAKE?

Experienced . . . . .Variable
Handy . . . . .Variable
Novice . . . . .Variable

VARIABLES: Time involved depends on the size and shape of the curved edge.

STUFF YOU'LL NEED

✔ **MATERIALS:**

Gravel, sand, edging, pavers, landscape spikes, clear lacquer, powdered chalk

✔ **TOOLS:**

Mason's line, garden hose or PVC pipe to lay out curve, tape measure, drysaw, power tamper, 3-pound sledgehammer, shovel, rake, knee pads, gloves, safety glasses, dust mask, hearing protection

Options for laying out curves

PVC PIPE is a low-tech tool. Hold the center of the pipe over the spot on the ground that will be the center of the curve. Have two helpers grab the ends and flex the pipe until it reaches the ends of the curve. It won't necessarily be a perfect arc, but it will be a smooth curve that connects the critical points along the edge of the patio.

A GARDEN HOSE is the perfect tool to form curves. Lay the hose on the ground in whatever shape you like, keeping the curves gentle. The smallest curve a masonry saw can cut is about 4 feet. Pick several key spots in the curve and measure their distance from each of the straight edges. You'll use the measurements later to re-create the curve.

1 **INSTALL EDGE RESTRAINTS ON TWO ADJOINING STRAIGHT SIDES.**
The curve may be the focal point, but the work begins on the straight sides. After you excavate for the patio and fill and level the foundation, put in edge restraints along two adjoining straight sides. Check that they're square using the 3-4-5 triangle method. (See page 38.)

2 **LAY OUT THE CURVE (ONE METHOD).** Lay out the curve with a compass made of mason's line, a landscape spike, and a squeeze bottle of powdered chalk. Using the compass will give you a perfect arc—each point on the curve will be the same distance from the center of the patio.

OPTIONS. Other methods mark the ground in a separate step. You can sprinkle chalk or flour along the pipe or hose to mark the ground. Gardeners like to lower the pH of the ground by marking it with lime. You can also buy marker spray paint, which comes in a can designed to be held upside down. It works well, but expect to get some on the hose.

3 **LAY THE PAVERS.** Start in a corner of the patio and lay pavers as you ordinarily would. Snap a few reference lines across the surface before you begin so you know if the pavers are staying in a straight line.

4 **CONTINUE PAST THE EDGE.** Don't try to cut the pavers to match the curve. Lay pavers so they either reach the layout or go just past it, as the pattern dictates. In a couple of steps, you will cut the curve while the pavers are on the ground.

5 **LAY OUT THE CURVE AGAIN.** Your work has covered up the layout line, which you'll need to cut the curve. Lay out the curve the way you did before and mark it in pencil, which gives you a more distinct cut line.

PATIOS

Laying a curved edge *(continued)*

6 **SPRAY WITH LACQUER.** Spray a clear lacquer over the layout line so it won't rub off before you finish cutting. The lacquer will wear off with use and when you compact the pavers into the sand bed.

7 **CUT WITH A DRYSAW.** Rent a drysaw with a diamond blade. If the saw has a hose connection for running water to cool the blade, don't use it. Run the saw dry so the water and concrete residue don't stain the pavers. The saw creates a lot of dust, so wear safety glasses and a mask. Avoid working when the wind will blow the dust through house windows or onto cars.

8 **INSTALL FLEXIBLE RESTRAINT.** After you cut the curve, put edge restraints around it immediately. Get flexible restraints and bend them to the shape of the curve, one short section at a time.

9 **SPREAD SAND AND COMPACT.** Spread sand across the surface of the pavers and compact it with a power tamper to fill the spaces between the pavers.

PATIOS

Laying a patio with an opening

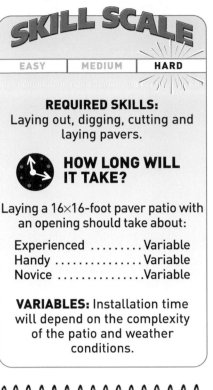
Because pavers are cast from concrete, they have uniform size and shape, which makes them easier to use than other materials when laying patios that have openings.

DETACHED PATIOS OFFER SECLUDED SPOTS FOR QUIET MOMENTS and can take advantage of views that may be different from the house. The addition of a fire ring makes this detached soft-set paver patio at least a three-season gathering place. Plantings around the edges could be added to create an opening, and a paver or gravel path could create access to the space from the house or other area.

The opening in this detached patio is for a center fire ring, but openings in patios can serve a number of functions and can be placed wherever you choose to put them. Consider adding flower boxes or low shrubbery in the corners or enclosing a tree to make it part of the patio space.

You'll need to know some special techniques for creating openings. Patio construction with a central opening such as this one starts at the opening and is laid out toward the edges. Edge restraints at the opening help keep the pavers in a straight line, but no restraints are in place along the edge of the patio at this point. They will be added when the patio is finished and trimmed. Ensuring that the pavers come out in the right spots and in straight lines requires special attention to layout. If it seems as if you are forever adjusting layout lines, taking them out, and then putting them back, it's because you are. However, if you aren't systematic about your layout, you may make a mistake—often one that can be fixed only by starting over. Working methodically, measuring carefully, and putting in accurate layout lines pay off.

No matter how you plan it, when you put down the last paver, the edges of the patio will be ragged. Trim them with a portable masonry saw, often called a drysaw, then put in the edge restraints. (See "Laying a Paver Patio," beginning on page 125, for more information.)

Laying a patio with an opening (continued)

1 **LAY OUT THE EDGES OF THE PATIO.** Lay out the edges of the patio with batterboards and mason's line as you ordinarily would. Double-check that opposite sides are parallel and that the corners meet at 90 degrees. This will probably mean adjusting and moving lines several times until the opening is square. (For more information, see "Layout," beginning on page 31.)

2 **TRANSFER THE LINES TO THE GROUND.** Sprinkle powdered chalk, lime, flour, or sand along the lines marking the edges of the patio. Lay out the opening, too, if it doesn't already exist. Excavate for the patio, digging an opening extending about a foot past the layout lines in each direction. Remove soil right up to the opening. Compact the soil with a power tamper and put down landscape fabric. Build up a 4-inch compacted gravel bed.

3 **PUT IN A SAND BED AND SCREED IT LEVEL.** Put a 1½-inch sand bed on top of the gravel. Temporarily put a couple of boards under the layout lines. Measure down at several points and shim as needed until they are the same distance below the line. Guide a notched board, or screed, across them to smooth the sand. (See "Laying a Paver Patio," beginning on page 125, for more information.)

4 **STRETCH A LINE ALONG ONE SIDE OF THE OPENING IN THE CENTER OF THE PATIO.** Determine the edges of the opening. If the patio is against a house or other structure, make the distance between the opening and house a multiple of the paver length to minimize cutting. The length and width of the opening also should be a multiple of the paver length. Set batterboards beyond the edges of the patio and stretch a line between them along one edge of the interior opening.

5 **STRETCH A PERPENDICULAR LINE.** Put in a second set of batterboards. Stretch a line between them that is perpendicular to the first and runs along the edge of the opening.

Make sure the batterboards are firmly set because you'll probably readjust the lines several times.

6 **CHECK FOR SQUARE.** If the opening isn't square, you'll have odd-shape spaces that a paver won't fill. Check the layout with a 3-4-5 triangle: Put a piece of tape 3 feet from where the lines cross along one line and another piece of tape 4 feet from where the lines cross on the other line. The layout is square if the distance between the pieces of tape is 5 feet. If not, slide the appropriate line along the batterboards until it is.

7 **STRETCH PARALLEL LINES.** Stretch lines over the remaining sides of the opening. Check that each is parallel with the line on the opposite side and double-check that they are square.

8 **MARK THE CORNERS.** Drop a plumb bob from the point where the lines meet at one corner of the patio. Mark the spot on the ground with a nail through a piece of paper for visibility. Repeat in each corner. Then drop a plumb bob from the lines marking the edge of the opening and mark where the lines meet the edges of the patio.

9 **SNAP LINES.** Snap a chalk line between nails on opposite corners of the patio. (Dry sand won't mark well, so you may want to mist the entire patio with a hose before you start your layout. If you still can't see the lines, stretch mason's line between the nails as a guide.) Snap lines marking all four edges of the patio and the opening. Remove the layout lines.

10 **PUT EDGE RESTRAINTS FOR THE INTERIOR OPENING,** following the lines you snapped. The upright face of the edging should be closest to the outside of the patio. Anchor the edging as directed by the manufacturer. For now don't put any edge restraints along the edge of the patio.

11 **SET UP A GUIDELINE.** Laying the pavers begins in the middle of this patio, where only a short edge restraint is in place to guide you. Stretch a line to keep the first row straight. Run it along the edge of the opening to the nails at the edge of the patio and stake it in place.

12 **START LAYING AT THE OPENING.** Lay pavers along the edge of the opening, aligning the ends of the pavers with the ends of the opening. Continue laying a row of pavers, following the line in one direction. When you reach the line marking the edge of the patio, lay the paver so that it either just meets the line or goes past it, as the pattern dictates. Repeat in the other direction.

Laying a patio with an opening *(continued)*

13 **LAY FROM THE OPENING TO THE EDGE OF THE PATIO.** Once the first row is in place, lay one next to it. Lay row by row until you reach the outer edge of the patio. Knee pads make the job more comfortable.

14 **LAY THE OTHER SIDE.** Go to the opposite side of the opening. Start laying pavers at the opening, aligning the ends of the pavers with the ends of opening. Lay pavers in this section of the patio the same way you did on the opposite side of the patio.

15 **FILL IN THE SIDES.** Starting at the edge restraints, fill in each gap on the remaining sides of the opening. A little adjustment may be necessary here, but if your layout lines were accurate, the pavers will fit.

16 **CUT THE EDGES.** Snap lines to mark the edges of the patio. Spray the lines with clear lacquer so they stay put as you work. Cut along the lines with a drysaw.

17 **INSTALL THE EDGING.** Put the edging tight against the pavers and fasten it as directed by the edging manufacturer.

18 **BED THE PAVERS.** Sweep sand over the patio and compact it into the joints, repeating until the joints are full.

PATIOS

Hard-bed patios, when properly installed, will last for generations. Pavers, bricks, or stones are laid over a concrete slab, and the joints are mortared, creating a bond that is practically indestructible.

A hard-bed patio resists shifting and cracking caused by seasonal changes and is a good solution in areas with severe climate fluctuations.

Although installing a hard-bed patio is more labor intensive and requires more steps than a soft-set installation, the result is a patio that is long-lasting and almost maintenance free.

If you're considering a hard-bed installation, it's important to research, design, and plan the project carefully. Hard-bed installations require some heavy lifting and attention to detail. Pouring the slab is hard work, but it's only the beginning—evaluate what's involved and make sure you're willing and able to do the entire project yourself.

Building a concrete patio

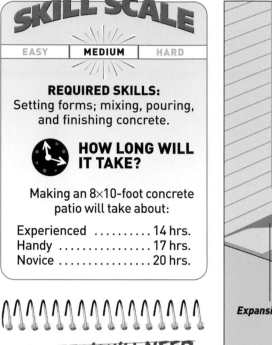

SKILL SCALE

EASY	**MEDIUM**	HARD

REQUIRED SKILLS:
Setting forms; mixing, pouring, and finishing concrete.

HOW LONG WILL IT TAKE?

Making an 8×10-foot concrete patio will take about:

Experienced . . . . 14 hrs.
Handy . . . . 17 hrs.
Novice . . . . 20 hrs.

STUFF YOU'LL NEED

✔ MATERIALS:
¾-inch gravel, 2× lumber, ½-inch plywood,10d (3-inch) duplex nails, ½-inch expansion joint, 6×6-10/10 wire mesh, tie wire, concrete, plastic sheeting, form-release agent

✔ TOOLS:
Mattock, spade, shovel, rake, tape measure, power tamper, hammer, 3-pound sledgehammer, mason's line, brick chisel, wheelbarrow, bull float, darby, edger, control jointer, pointing trowel, magnesium float, broom, safety goggles, work gloves, paintbrush

Designer Tip

FINISHING TOUCHES
A broomed surface is skid resistant and easy to apply. Other surfaces, such as exposed aggregate, are more attractive and also skid resistant. For more on surface treatments, see "Special Surface Finishes," page 96.

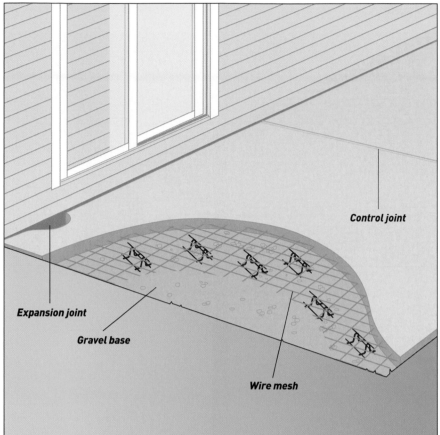

Control joint

Expansion joint

Gravel base

Wire mesh

A CONCRETE PATIO IS A SYSTEM OF STONE, METAL, AND CONCRETE. The top 4 inches is a concrete slab. A wire mesh running through the middle of the pad ties the patio together. Beneath the concrete is a gravel bed, which improves drainage and is easier to level than soil. An expansion joint between the patio and any structure allows the two to move separately when the ground shifts. Forms hold the concrete in place when you pour it. They also act as guides—immediately after you pour the concrete, you drag a board across the forms to level the surface. The forms usually are removed after the concrete cures, but you can leave them in place as decorative trim.

The base of rigid patios—mortared brick, mortared flagstone, tile, or concrete—is a concrete pad. Concrete provides a solid base beneath these materials. It also prevents them from cracking as the ground shifts from temperature changes.

In most areas a concrete patio begins with 4 inches of compacted stone. Areas with excellent drainage don't require a stone base—check with your local building inspector's office to see what's required. A 4-inch concrete slab is laid on the stone.

The following instructions are for building a concrete patio on grade. The steps are the same if you build a base for a rigid patio.

The difference is the depth you dig before you pour. If you install a concrete patio, dig out a space 8 inches deep—4 inches for the stone and another 4 inches for the concrete. If you install a brick patio, the base will need to be about 10 inches deep—4 inches for the stone, 4 inches for the concrete, and another 2 inches to allow for mortar and brick. If you build in brick, stone, or tile, simply read how the pad is poured. You'll find information on setting the pad at the right depth in later projects.

ASSEMBLING FORMS

1 **LAY OUT AND EXCAVATE THE PATIO.** Lay out the patio with batterboards and mason's line. Remove the sod, dig out 8 inches of soil, and compact the exposed surface. Spread gravel on the surface in 2-inch layers, compacting each layer and adding gravel for a bed 4 inches deep.

2 **LAY OUT THE OUTSIDE EDGE OF THE FORMS.** Install a second set of layout lines on stakes. Position the stakes outside the first set of lines, offset from the first set by the width of the forms you'll use. Level the lines with a line level or water level.

3 **DRIVE STAKES ALONG THE NEW LAYOUT LINES.** Drive stakes along the layout lines, putting them at the corners of the patio and every 2 feet in between. Drive the stakes straight up and down, firmly embedding them in the ground. Trim them to height later.

4 **MARK THE STAKES.** The patio must slope away from the house at a rate of ⅛ to ¼ inch per foot—check local code for the proper rate. Measure down from the batterboards and mark the two end stakes at the finished height of the patio. Hold a chalk line tight at the marks you made and snap it to mark the rest of the stakes.

Building a concrete patio

ASSEMBLING FORMS *(continued)*

5 **NAIL THE FIRST FORM IN PLACE.** Align a 2×4 with the marks on the stakes and nail it in place with two duplex nails. Brace the form board with a 3-pound sledgehammer while you pound in the nails. Nail the rest of the stakes to the form board the same way.

Using a sledgehammer to brace the forms while you nail the stakes to them will absorb the shock of the hammer and help keep the stakes firmly planted in the ground. Loose forms can create uneven edges.

6 **CUT OFF THE STAKES.** Cut the stakes flush with or slightly below the tops of the forms. You will use the tops as a guide to level the surface of the concrete, and any stake sticking above the surface will keep you from getting a smooth surface.

7 **INSTALL THE REMAINING FORMS.** Cut a 2×4 long enough to span each of the remaining sides. Put each board in place so the top is level with the marks you made earlier on the stakes. Attach stakes to forms with duplex nails. Nail in the remaining forms.

PATIOS

8 **SPLICE BOARDS TOGETHER, IF NECESSARY.** On sides too long for a single board, butt two boards together. Cut a strip of ½-inch plywood and nail it across the joint. Drive a 2×4 stake at each end of the plywood strip and nail it to the form with duplex nails.

9 **INSTALL THE EXPANSION JOINT.** Place a ½×4-inch expansion joint against the foundation of the house and any other existing concrete that meets the patio. This will prevent the pad and foundation from bonding and then cracking if they settle at different rates.

10 **COAT THE FORMS WITH RELEASE AGENT.** Coat the form boards with a coat of commercial release agent or vegetable oil to prevent the concrete from sticking to the form boards. Motor oil—an early substitute for the release agent—doesn't work as well and contaminates the ground.

Designer Tip

11 **PLACE THE MESH.** Reinforce the concrete with 6×6-10/10 wire mesh (6-inch squares of 10-gauge metal). Put the mesh on wire supports, sold separately, so it sits roughly in the middle of the slab's thickness. Leave a few inches of space between the mesh and the edges of the forms to prevent rust. Overlap sections by 4 inches and tie them together with wire. Wire the mesh to the supports.

MIXED MEDIA

Break up the bland look of a concrete patio with a grid of permanent form boards. Install the boards just like temporary forms but pound the stakes below the top of the forms so the poured concrete will conceal them. If you want to stain the wood, soak the boards in the finish first, then cover the wood with masking tape when you make the pour.

Building a concrete patio (continued)

POURING CONCRETE

WORK SMARTER

POURING CONCRETE
Pour concrete into the forms as close as possible to its final position and dump each wheelbarrow load against the previous load. If you don't, the cement and sand will ooze away from the gravel in the mix, and you'll get rough and smooth spots in the surface. Start by pouring the concrete into a corner, and then work your way along the form, as shown in Step 1. Once you've dumped concrete along the entire edge, move your ramp to the other side of the patio. Extend the ramp across the patio so that you can get as close as possible to the concrete you've already poured, and start pouring new concrete against it. Running the ramp, or the wheelbarrow, along the reinforcing mesh will cause the mesh to bend, but don't worry. It's unavoidable. Pull bent mesh back up in place with a rake just before you pour concrete over it.

1 **POUR THE CONCRETE INTO THE FORMS.** If you're using a wheelbarrow, build a temporary ramp over the forms so that the wheelbarrow won't knock them out of place. Start in a corner and dump the loads of concrete against each other. Have a helper with a shovel spread the concrete into corners and against the forms and expansion joints.

2 **REMOVE TRAPPED AIR.** Lay a wide board across the forms so you can reach the interior of the pour. If the concrete causes the wire mesh to sink, pull it up with a rake so that it's in the middle of the slab. Work a shovel or rake up and down to remove air pockets, especially alongside the forms.

3 **FLATTEN THE SURFACE.** With a helper pull a screed (a long, straight 2×4) across the forms to level the concrete. Tilt the screed forward and slide it from side to side as you push it forward. Shovel off excess concrete in front of the screed or fill in low spots. Make a second pass with the screed tilted the opposite direction.

4 **FLOAT THE CONCRETE.** Work a bull float back and forth with the blade flat against the surface to smooth and compact the concrete. For small surfaces use a darby instead of a bull float. Work the concrete until water forms on the surface.

WORK SMARTER

SCRATCHING THE SURFACE
If you're going to lay bricks or pavers on top of a concrete patio, make sure it's flat but don't spend a lot of time getting a smooth finish. Instead you'll need to scratch the surface to help the mortar bond to the concrete. Begin by building a homemade scarifier. Drive 10d (3-inch) nails 1 inch apart into a piece of scrap wood. Then drag the scarifier over the concrete before it sets fully, cutting grooves into the surface.

PATIOS

FINISHING CONCRETE

1 **ROUND THE EDGES.** When you've finished floating, separate the concrete from the forms by running the tip of a pointing trowel between the two. Then slide the cutting edge of an edger along the forms to round over the patio edge, making it less likely to chip. Lift the leading edge of the tool to avoid marring the concrete.

2 **CUT CONTROL JOINTS.** Cut shallow grooves, called control joints, in the wet cement pad. These weaken the spots a little so that if the ground shifts, the resulting crack should form along the control joint. You need a joint every 8 feet, so make marks every 8 feet along the forms. Place a jointer at each mark. Guide the jointer against a board that spans the patio. Control joints can also be cut after the concrete has cured using a circular saw with a cement or masonry blade. (See inset.)

Designer Tip

FINISH OPTIONS

Function often dictates how a patio should be finished. For a smoother finish, use a magnesium float instead of a wooden one. Avoid finishing concrete with a steel trowel because it will create a finish so smooth that it becomes slick and dangerous when wet. A skid-free, broomed finish is an especially good idea around pools.

PATIOS

3 **FLOAT THE SURFACE AGAIN.** After cutting the control joints, and when any water sheen has left the surface, run a wood or magnesium hand float over the surface to provide a final smoothing. Raise the leading edge of the float slightly as you work to avoid making lines on the surface of the concrete.

4 **BRUSH THE SURFACE.** For improved traction, pull a stiff-bristle broom across the surface. Draw the broom in either straight or wavy lines. If you don't like the pattern or if it is too coarse, trowel, wait, and broom again. The longer the concrete dries, the finer the broomed surface. Make another pass along the perimeter with the edger.

5 **LET THE CONCRETE CURE.** Lay plastic sheeting over the finished surface. The moisture trapped inside eliminates the need for watering during the curing stage. Let the concrete cure at least 48 hours, then remove the form boards. (For more on curing concrete, see page 93.)

Preparing an existing slab for a mortar bed

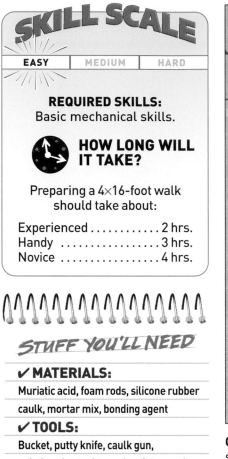

SKILL SCALE

EASY	MEDIUM	HARD

REQUIRED SKILLS:
Basic mechanical skills.

HOW LONG WILL IT TAKE?

Preparing a 4×16-foot walk should take about:

Experienced . . . . 2 hrs.
Handy . . . . 3 hrs.
Novice . . . . 4 hrs.

STUFF YOU'LL NEED

✔ **MATERIALS:**

Muriatic acid, foam rods, silicone rubber caulk, mortar mix, bonding agent

✔ **TOOLS:**

Bucket, putty knife, caulk gun, paintbrush, steel trowel, safety goggles, rubber gloves, work gloves

Steps are cracks that have shifted so much that one surface is higher than the other. Steps can cause problems because they are likely to appear again and may mean that the pad has to be removed and repoured.

Consult a professional landscape or concrete contractor to make sure the steps won't reappear, this time through your new patio.

CRACKS AND SHIFTING OCCUR NATURALLY IN CONCRETE SLABS. Even the best-laid slabs will eventually be affected by years of seasonal changes and freeze/thaw cycles. Repairing cracks and covering an existing slab with mortared bricks or pavers adds a design element to your yard and saves you the labor of removing damaged concrete.

A new patio doesn't necessarily mean you need to pour a new slab. In many cases you can apply brick, stone, or tile over an existing slab. You'll need to patch and clean it, but it's considerably less work than starting from scratch.

Control joints in the concrete can cause cracking in the surface above them, so tile and brick work best on an old surface. Lay out the brick or tile so a mortar joint is directly above the control joint, and fill the joint with caulk instead of mortar or grout.

First make sure the existing slab is sound. Cracks and irregularities can be repaired, as can a few small areas that have broken away. Make sure the area is flat—if a crack has created a step in the surface, it will crack again after you patch it, and the crack will eventually work its way through the brick, stone, or tile.

Crumbling areas spell big trouble: Either the concrete was poorly mixed or multiple freeze/thaw cycles have broken the surface. If the slab surface is crumbling, talk to a mason about whether the pad can be repaired.

Check that the surface of the slab slopes away from the house at a rate of at least ⅛ inch per foot. If it doesn't you can correct the problem by sloping the forms when you apply the mortar.

Etch the concrete surface with a mixture of muriatic acid and water to clean it and create a surface to which mortar will stick. Make sure you add the acid to the water—not the water to the acid—to avoid dangerous splashes.

Ensure a good bond for the mortar and brick, stone, or tile by applying a bonding agent.

1 **CLEAN THE SURFACE.** Scrape off gum, wax, and dirt. Carefully mix five parts water and one part muriatic acid, adding the acid to the water to avoid dangerous splashes. Carefully pour the solution on the slab. Rinse the slab thoroughly with fresh water.

2 **FILL IN THE CONTROL JOINTS.** Patch broken or wide control joints by pushing foam backing rods below the surface with a putty knife. Seal the crack with a silicone rubber caulk. If you are laying brick or tile on top of the concrete, put the mortar joint directly above the control joint to avoid cracking.

3 **FILL IN CRACKS.** Brush a concrete bonding agent on an area 6 inches wider and longer than the crack. Then fill the crack with mortar and level it with a steel trowel.

4 **APPLY A BONDING AGENT.** Just before you apply mortar, brush on a coat of concrete bonding adhesive to the entire surface, following the directions on the package.

5 **REGRADE THE AREA AROUND THE PAD.** Once you install the brick, stone, or tile, the surface of the patio will be above the adjacent ground surface. Regrade the area, adding soil and raking it smooth until it is flush with the patio surface.

A+ WORK SMARTER

CORRECTING THE SLOPE
You can add a bed of mortar up to 4 inches thick to a patio without compromising the strength. Take advantage of this method to correct any problems with the existing patio's slope. First build forms around the patio the way you would if you were pouring a new patio, keeping the surface as low as possible while making sure the forms have the correct slope. Fill the forms with mortar and pull a screed across it to flatten it. Let the mortar cure, then lay the stone, brick, or tile, following the directions beginning on page 150.

PATIOS

Laying a mortared brick patio

Bricks can be laid directly on a sand-and-gravel base (page 132), but for a long-lasting patio, lay the bricks on a concrete base. The glue that holds bricks to concrete—and bricks to bricks—is mortar, a mix of portland cement, lime, sand, and water. Use Type M mortar—it's designed for outdoor use.

A word about bricks: A 4×8-inch brick is narrower by the width of the intended joint between bricks. Rounding up makes calculating brick amounts easier, but if you use the wrong joint size, laying some patterns becomes impossible. As a rule, if the brick is shy of its named size by ½ inch, use ½-inch joints; if shy by ⅜ inch, use ⅜-inch joints. If it measures a full 4×8 inches, get another brick.

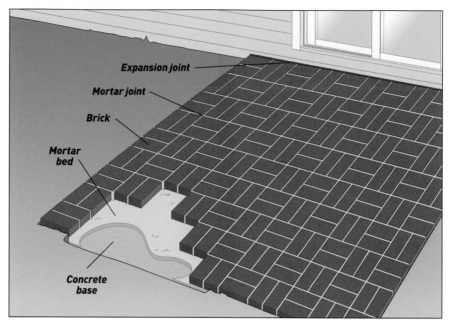

Expansion joint
Mortar joint
Brick
Mortar bed
Concrete base

A MORTARED BRICK PATIO IS ESSENTIALLY A SERIES OF LAYERS. A concrete foundation supports the bricks and establishes the slope that directs water away from the house. The exact depth of the foundation varies, but it's positioned so the patio is about 2 inches above ground. A ½-inch layer of mortar applied to the top of the concrete holds the bricks in place. Once the bricks are laid, you apply more mortar between them and shape, or "strike," it with a jointer.

SKILL SCALE

EASY	**MEDIUM**	HARD

REQUIRED SKILLS:
Basic to intermediate masonry skills.

HOW LONG WILL IT TAKE?

Laying an 8×10-foot brick patio on a concrete base will take about:

Experienced .... 10 hrs.
Handy .... 14 hrs.
Novice .... 18 hrs.

STUFF YOU'LL NEED

✔ **MATERIALS:**
2× lumber, 10d (3-inch) duplex nails, mortar, bricks

✔ **TOOLS:**
Mason's line, 3-pound sledgehammer, hammer, mixing tub, mason's trowel, rubber mallet, circular saw and masonry blade, brick chisel, mortar bag, jointer, concave jointer, safety glasses, work gloves, dust mask

MORTARING BRICKS

1 **SET MASON'S LINES** at the finished height and slope of the patio. Set form boards so the tops are ½ inch above the slab surface. Add corner stakes to support the forms and drive them in until they are flush with the form boards. Nail stakes every 2 feet against the boards.

2 **POUR A BAG OF PRE-MIXED TYPE M MORTAR** into a mixing tub or wheelbarrow. Make a small well in the middle and pour in water, a bit at a time. (The instructions give you the approximate amount.) Mix with a trowel. The mortar is the right consistency when it is firm enough to cling to a trowel turned on edge.

3 **DIVIDE THE PATIO INTO SECTIONS**
4 feet wide with a temporary pipe or board the same height as the top of the forms. Throw mortar into an area roughly 4×4 feet. Make a screed from a straight 2×4 that spans the width of the forms. Draw the screed over the mortar to level and smooth it into a ½-inch bed.

4 **FOR A BASKET-WEAVE PATTERN**
lay the first pair of bricks in a corner even with the inside edge of the forms. Space the bricks with a spacer. Tap the bricks firmly into the mortar with a rubber mallet.

SAFETY ALERT

Wear a dust mask and safety glasses when cutting bricks.

5 **IF YOU WORK ON A LARGE PATIO,**
run a mason's line across it, flush with the top of the first two courses, to keep the bricks properly aligned. Lay a pair of bricks perpendicular to the first two. Continue laying the bricks, alternating their direction.

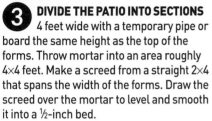

6 **CHECK FOR HIGH AND LOW SPOTS**
as you proceed by placing a 2×4 across the bricks. Put mortar under low bricks; seat high ones by tapping them with the mallet. Lay another 4×4-foot patch of mortar and bricks, repeating until the patio is finished.

7 **WHEN A BRICK HAS TO BE CUT,**
score it ⅛ inch deep with a circular saw with a masonry blade. Once the brick is scored, cut it with a solid blow from a brick chisel and a 3-pound sledgehammer.

8 **WHEN ALL THE BRICKS ARE SET IN THE MORTAR BED,** fill the joints between bricks with mortar from a mortar bag, also called a blow bag. Working back and forth, squeeze the mortar carefully into the joints until they are filled. Shape the joints with a concave jointer.

HARD-BED PATIOS 151

Laying a mortared brick patio

MORTARING BRICKS (continued)

9 **CLEAN THE BRICK.** Be careful not to get mortar on the brick. Remove any mortar that does get on the brick by rubbing it with a piece of wet burlap. Let the mortar cure for three days before using the patio. If you missed any mortar spots, you can usually remove them by sweeping wet sand over them.

Laying dry-mortar joints

As its name suggests, dry mortar contains no water. You simply sweep it into the joints. Mix four parts sand and one part dry portland cement and sweep the mixture into the joints with a stiff brush. Then spray the patio—and especially the joints—with water. While the joints are still damp, shape each one with a concave jointer. Once the mortar has hardened for a few hours, scrub the patio surface to remove any excess mortar.

SELECTING A BRICK PATTERN

RUNNING BOND IS THE EASIEST TO LAY. Every second row begins with a half brick to stagger the joints. (For directions on laying running bond, see page 56.)

HERRINGBONE REQUIRES A LITTLE MORE PLANNING than running bond. It can be laid either diagonally or parallel to the sides of the patio. (For directions on laying herringbone, see pages 58–59.)

Designer Tip

PATTERN POSSIBILITIES
You aren't limited to just one pattern when you lay bricks. You can create interesting effects by combining two patterns on the same patio. Start with a basket-weave pattern, for example, then lay a couple of rows of running bond before resuming the basket-weave pattern. Experiment on paper first to make sure the overall pattern looks good.

PATIOS

Laying a mortared stone patio

Stone for patios is sold under various names, such as flagstone, flat stone, and bluestone. Whatever the name, choose a natural, sedimentary, layered rock. Although you can buy stones precut, the patio style shown here uses rough, natural stone laid with gaps of ½ or ¾ inch between stones. This patio slopes for drainage and is supported by a concrete foundation.

SKILL SCALE

EASY	MEDIUM	**HARD**

REQUIRED SKILLS:
Laying a stone patio is heavy work that requires basic to intermediate masonry skills.

 HOW LONG WILL IT TAKE?

Laying stones on a mortared bed to make an 8×10-foot patio will take about:

Experienced .... 12 hrs.
Handy .... 16 hrs.
Novice .... 20 hrs.

STUFF YOU'LL NEED

✔ **MATERIALS:**
2× lumber, 10d (3-inch) duplex nails, mortar, stones

✔ **TOOLS:**
Hammer, 3-pound sledgehammer, brick chisel, carpenter's pencil, pointing trowel, mason's trowel, grout bag, rubber mallet, concave jointer, sponge, shovel, safety glasses, work gloves, dust mask, mixing tub

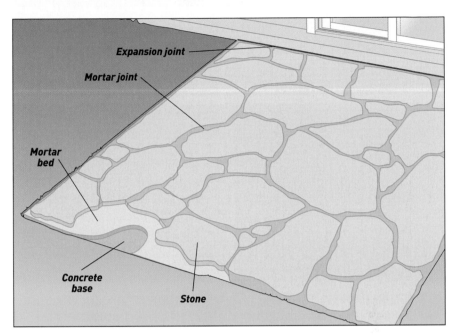

Expansion joint
Mortar joint
Mortar bed
Concrete base
Stone

BECAUSE OF THE UNEVEN NATURE OF STONE, a stone patio sits in a relatively thick 1-inch bed of mortar. Temporary forms hold the wet mortar in place. You'll drag a board across the forms to smooth the bed, so set the forms to follow the desired slope of the patio. The concrete pad under the patio supports it and keeps it from cracking when the ground underneath it shifts. To help the stones adhere to the mortar, coat them with slurry, a mixture of cement and water that has the consistency of cream.

1 BUILD FORMS FOR THE MORTAR. Put 2× forms around the concrete slab to hold the mortar bed. The forms should sit 1 inch above the slab and follow its slope. Hold the forms in place with stakes driven every 2 feet.

2 LAY OUT THE STONES. Lay a dry run of stones on the patio. The best way to do this is to randomly spread the large stones across the patio and then fill in with smaller ones. Group the stones so there is as little space as possible between them. Inevitable empty spots are OK.

Laying a mortared stone patio *(continued)*

3 **FILL IN THE VOIDS.** Place large stones over the voids. Use a pencil to sketch the shape required to fill the void.

A carpenter's pencil makes a more visible line than a regular pencil.

4 **CUT THE STONE.** Chip away at the stones with the pointed end of a mason's hammer to cut the shape. To cut a straight line, score the line with a 3-pound sledgehammer and a brick chisel. Place the scored line over the edge of a piece of 1×2 or a pipe. Sever with a solid blow from the sledgehammer.

5 **NUMBER THE STONES.** Once the stones fit, number the bottoms and lay them out in order next to the patio.

6 **MIX MORTAR.** Pour a bag of pre-mixed Type M mortar into a mixing tub. Make a small well in the middle. Pour water into the well, a little at a time, and mix with the trowel. The mix may take slightly more or less water than called for by the manufacturer. It is the right consistency when it is firm enough to cling to a trowel turned on edge.

7 **SPREAD A SMALL AMOUNT OF MORTAR.** Using a mason's trowel, lay a 1-inch mortar bed for two or three stones at a time. Use the forms to help lay the right amount of mortar. Screed it with a straight 2×4 that spans the width of the forms. (If laid stones obstruct screeding, guide the screed along two 1-inch O.D. {outside diameter} pipes temporarily set on the slab.)

8 **LAY THE STONES.** Place the first stone in the mortar and embed it firmly in place by tapping it with a rubber mallet. Lay adjoining stones, referring to the numbers on the bottom to help reposition them in the proper order. Check for high and low spots as you proceed by laying a 2×4 on top of the stones.

PATIOS

9 **LEVEL AND COAT WITH SLURRY.**
Add mortar to raise stones that are too low; tap harder to set those that are too high. After laying stones in about a 4×4-foot section, tip the stones up one at a time and paint the bottom with a cream-textured cement-water slurry mixture. Lay the stones back in place and recheck their level.

10 **LAY THE REST OF THE PATIO.**
Continue laying the patio in 4×4-foot sections. Make a dry run for each section, number the stones, then set them in mortar. When you finish, let the mortar cure for one or two days. Then remove the temporary forms around the patio.

11 **MORTAR BETWEEN THE STONES.**
Mix another batch of Type M mortar. Pack it between the stones with a pointing trowel.

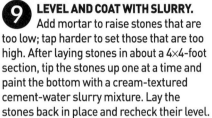

12 **TOOL THE JOINTS.** Compress and smooth the mortar joints with a ¾-inch brick jointer. Remove any mortar crumbs from the joint edges.

13 **REMOVE MORTAR FROM THE STONES.** After a few hours clean up any mortar on the stones with a damp sponge or a rough burlap rag and water.

14 **COVER THE PATIO WITH PLASTIC.**
Wait 24 hours for the mortar to cure. Remove the plastic and backfill the edges around the patio with soil. Tamp the soil and reseed or plant.

Laying a tile patio

SKILL SCALE

EASY | **MEDIUM** | HARD

REQUIRED SKILLS:
Basic masonry skills.

HOW LONG WILL IT TAKE?

Installing a 10×10-foot tile patio will take:

Experienced ....3.5 hrs.
Handy ....4.5 hrs.
Novice ....5.5 hrs.

VARIABLES: Installation times will be affected by delivery of materials, complexity of design, weather conditions, and curing times.

STUFF YOU'LL NEED

✔ **MATERIALS:**
Tile, tile spacers, mortar, grout, tile sealer

✔ **TOOLS:**
Tape measure, chalk line, 5-gallon bucket, ½-inch drill, mortar paddle, notched trowel, rubber gloves, sponge, rags, sponge mop, bead blaster, tile saw or snap cutter, grout float

Adding ß tile to a concrete pad will create a distinctive addition to your outdoor living space. Be sure and choose a tile rated to survive freeze/thaw cycles in Northern climates.

Ceramic tile patios are popular in the southern United States, where they're used along with indoor tile to bridge the gap between indoors and out. But ceramic tile makers say there's no reason not to build tile patios in the north too.

The first step—no matter where you live—is to purchase the right tile. You can find out what you need to know by reading a series of icons and labels on the tile cartons. For all floor uses, get tile rated Grade 1, which is designed for floors. Grade 2 has imperfections; Grade 3 tiles are wall tiles and will crack on floors.

Look for tile that has :
- **PEI (Porcelain Enamel Institute) Wear Rating 3,** meaning it's for residential use.

- **WA (water absorption) rating of 5 percent or less.** This keeps the inside of the tile dry enough to prevent freezing.

- **COF (coefficient of friction) rating of .60 or less,** meaning it has some texture for traction. Double-check by running your hand across the surface.

- **Frost resistance.** Look for a snowflake icon that indicates the tile will survive the freeze/thaw cycle.

The next step is to get the latex-modified mortar; the latex helps keep water from working its way into the mortar, where it can freeze and loosen the tile. The farther north you live, the more latex needed. Ask at the store about what's right for the job in your area.

Set tile on concrete. If you pour a new pad, give it a broomed finish that the mortar can grab on to. If you tile an existing pad, it probably has a smooth steel trowel finish and probably was coated with a curing compound after it was poured. Either will keep the mortar from forming a firm bond with the concrete, causing the tile to come loose. To solve the problem, rent a bead blaster to rough up the surface.

1 **PREPARE THE CONCRETE.** Rough up the surface of the concrete and remove any sealer or curing compound with a bead blaster. Slowly push the blaster across the floor as it shoots metal balls at the floor and vacuums them up. The impact will wear off any coatings and create a rough surface for the mortar.

2 **SNAP LAYOUT LINES.** Snap chalk lines at the middle of opposite sides. Measure 3 feet from the intersection along one line and 4 feet along the other line. If the distance between the points is 5 feet, the lines are square. If not, reposition one of the lines until it is square with the other. (See page 38.)

3 **TEST-FIT THE TILES.** When you buy tiles, buy spacers the size of the mortar joint. Starting where the lines cross, put tiles along each line with plastic spacers between them. If any of the tiles along the edges are less than half a tile wide, snap a new line to solve the problem.

Buy spacers in the tile section and insert them on edge between the tiles for easy removal.

4 **MIX THE MORTAR.** Add about half the water called for on the mortar box or bag. Slowly add the rest while mixing at slow speed with a paddle designed for mortar (not paint). After mixing let the mortar rest for 10 minutes, then mix again before use.

5 **SPREAD THE MORTAR.** Start at the intersection of the chalk lines and spread mortar over an 8- to 10-square-foot area. Press the mortar into the slab with a trowel held at a shallow angle.

6 **COMB THE MORTAR.** Comb the mortar in straight lines, holding the trowel at a 45-degree angle to the slab and forcing the teeth of the trowel against the concrete. This ensures you have the right amount of mortar on the concrete. The size of the notch should equal the thickness of the tile.

HARD-BED PATIOS 157

Laying a tile patio *(continued)*

(continued)

7 **LAY THE FIRST TILE.** Start at the intersection of the lines, put the tile in the mortar, and twist it slightly to embed it in the mortar.

Leave a space the size of a grout joint between the tile and any structure.

8 **CHECK THE BACK.** Pull up the tile and look at the back. Parallel mortar lines mean the bed isn't thick enough; dry areas mean the mortar is too old. In either event scrape up the mortar and reapply. If the bed was too thin, hold the trowel at a greater angle when you comb out the mortar.

9 **WORK YOUR WAY ACROSS THE MORTAR.** When the mortar bed is right, lay the first two tiles and a couple of spacers placed on end between them. Lay all the tiles in the mortared area. Lay a short 2×4 on top of the tiles and lightly tap with a rubber mallet to level the tiles.

10 **LAY THE REST OF THE FLOOR.** Lay mortar over an area the same size as the first and set tiles in it. Check the back of a tile occasionally to make sure you're laying enough mortar. Work area by area until you tile the entire patio.

11 **CUT TILES TO FIT ALONG THE EDGE OF THE PATIO.** At the edge of the patio, you'll probably need to cut tiles to fit. Mark where you need to make cuts and cut with either a tile saw or a snap cutter.

Using a snap cutter

To use a snap cutter, place the tile with the cutting wheel on top of the layout line, then move the wheel back toward the far edge of the tile. Pull the wheel toward you, putting light pressure on the handle. Lower the foot of the cutter onto the tile and strike the handle quickly to snap along the scored line.

PATIOS

APPLYING GROUT

1 **MIX AND APPLY GROUT.** Remove the spacers. Mix the grout at slow speed in a 5-gallon bucket with a mortar paddle and a ½-inch drill. Let the grout rest for 10 to 15 minutes, then remix.

2 **SPREAD THE GROUT.** Apply the grout with a rubber grout float held at a shallow angle. Press the grout into the joints to fill them. For joints wider than ⅜ inch, use a grout bag. Fill the joints between the patio and any structures with caulk instead of grout.

3 **REMOVE EXCESS GROUT.** Hold the grout float at a steep angle. Diagonally sweep the float across the tiles so the float doesn't dip into the joints.

4 **RINSE, RINSE, AND RINSE AGAIN.** Immediately wash off the haze left by the grout before it dries. Rinse repeatedly and keep the water clean in order to remove the haze.

5 **MIST THE GROUT.** Let the grout damp cure by spraying it with a mist (don't drench it) several times a day for three days. If the patio receives direct sunlight, cover it with plastic sheeting between mistings.

6 **APPLY SEALER.** Check the directions that come with the sealer to see how long you should wait before applying it. Apply the sealer with a sponge mop and wipe up the excess before it dries. Follow the manufacturer's directions for the number of applications.

13 STEPS AND RAMPS

PATIOS

Steps and ramps are connectors that provide transition from one level to another while adding a strong design element. Ramps offer an easy means of moving from one level to another, especially important for physically challenged people.

Choose the materials for your steps to complement the installation. Bricks or pavers offer color and a sense of order, while rough stone creates a free-form look and blends with the surrounding landscape. Combining timbers and brick to make steps adds texture and a dynamic architectural element to any setting.

Practically speaking, be sure that risers and treads are balanced in height and width so they are comfortable to walk up and down at a normal pace. Steps that are too narrow and too short encourage slips and falls. Ensure that edges are clearly visible. Not being able to discern where a step ends is a prime cause of accidents.

Laying out steps

How much room does your foot need for each step? And how high should you have to raise your foot to get to the next step?

Here's a formula for the ideal relationship between the height of the step (the rise) and the depth (the run). Twice the rise plus the run should equal 25 to 27 inches. This formula results in steps that are less steep than steps indoors but more comfortable to climb. You'll appreciate less steep steps when trudging through snow or hauling firewood up the slope.

When you plan your steps, plan for the top step to be level with the grade so people can see it easily as they approach.

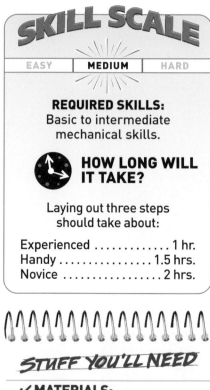

SKILL SCALE

EASY	**MEDIUM**	HARD

REQUIRED SKILLS:
Basic to intermediate mechanical skills.

HOW LONG WILL IT TAKE?

Laying out three steps should take about:

Experienced . . . . 1 hr.
Handy . . . . 1.5 hrs.
Novice . . . . 2 hrs.

STUFF YOU'LL NEED

✔ MATERIALS:
2×4s, 2×2s, galvanized 10d (3-inch) nails, masking tape

✔ TOOLS:
Tape measure, 3-pound sledgehammer, mason's line, line level, plumb bob, powdered chalk, framing square, spade, level, tamper

CALCULATING RISER/TREAD RATIOS

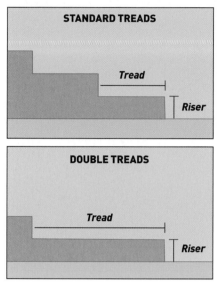

STANDARD TREADS

Tread

Riser

DOUBLE TREADS

Tread

Riser

Riser height:	Tread range:
Standard Treads	
7"	11-13"
6½"	12-14"
6"	13-15"
5½"	14-16"
5"	15-17"
Double Treads	
7"	22-26"
6½"	24-28"
6"	26-30"
5½"	28-32"
5"	30-34"

CHANGING THE NUMBER OF STEPS ON A HILL CHANGES BOTH THE SIZE OF THE TREAD AND THE RISE BETWEEN TREADS. Some combinations make more comfortable climbing than others. The chart above shows you the most comfortable combinations of tread and rise for both single- and double-tread stairs. The step-by-step directions guide you through the decisionmaking process.

Planning stairs with a sixteen-inch total rise and a 60-inch run

1) CALCULATE THE NUMBER OF RISERS. Divide the total rise (16 inches) by the riser height you've chosen (use 6 inches as an example) to find the number of risers (2⅔). Round up to the nearest whole number (3), if necessary.

2) CALCULATE THE ACTUAL SIZE OF THE RISER. If you had to round up to get the actual number of steps, you'll have to recalculate the rise they require. Divide the total rise by the number of risers to get the actual rise. In this case the actual rise is 5⅓ inches.

3) CALCULATE THE DEPTH OF THE TREAD. Steps have an equal number of risers and treads—three of each in the example. Divide the total run by the number of steps to get the distance from the front to the back of each step. In this case the steps will be 20 inches deep making a run of 60 inches.

4) SKETCH OUT YOUR STAIRS. Make a rough drawing of your stairs to use while you work. Draw in the rise, run, riser height, and size of the treads. Double-check your math by adding the numbers. The combined height of the risers should equal the total rise. The combined size of the treads should equal the total run.

Laying out steps

LAYING OUT AND EXCAVATING

1 **SET UP STAKES AND LINE.** Drive 2×2 stakes into the ground at the top and bottom of the slope a little beyond the ends of the steps. Drive a tall stake at the bottom of the slope. Run a mason's line from the base of the top stake to the bottom stake along what will be one edge of the steps and level it with a line level.

2 **LAY OUT THE LENGTH OF THE STAIRS.** Choose the points on the ground where you want the stairway to start and stop. Mark them on the mason's line with masking tape.

3 **MEASURE THE RISE.** Stand at the bottom of the slope and measure the distance from the line to the ground in inches. The distance is the total rise of the stairway.

4 **MEASURE THE RUN.** Have a helper stand at the top of the hill holding one end of a tape measure while you stand at the bottom holding the other end. Measure along the line in inches to find out the run of the stairs.

WORK SMARTER

IF THE SHOE WON'T FIT

If the risers and treads don't meet the standards for comfort (see page 161), recalculate using a different riser height. If you still can't get what you want, make the stairway longer or shorter. A longer stairway results in shorter rises. A shorter stairway results in higher rises.

If you build steps on a short, steep slope, finding an acceptable riser/tread ratio sometimes can be challenging. One solution is to construct the steps at an angle to the slope rather than build them straight up and down the slope, building—in effect—a longer stairway.

Work slowly and carefully when excavating. Use your legs as you lift the shovel to protect your back from strain and possible injury.

9 LAY OUT THE STEPS ON THE GROUND. Once you calculate the number and size of the risers and treads, make any required adjustments to your layout stakes and mason's line. Then measure along the mason's line and tape where each tread will begin. Transfer the marks to the ground with a plumb bob and powdered chalk.

10 LAY OUT THE WALK. Lower the mason's line to just above the ground, then mark the opposite edge of the steps with a parallel line. Lay out the front of each tread with stakes and line, intersecting the lines at the marks on the ground. Use a framing square to make sure corners are perfectly square.

11 DOUBLE-CHECK FOR SQUARE. Double-check for square by measuring the diagonals of the overall layout—they will be equal if the layout is square. Check that the individual steps are square, too, and make any necessary adjustments.

12 DIG OUT THE FIRST STEP. Remove the sod and dig a rough step in the soil. At the back of the step, dig down the thickness of the paving material. Dig far enough past the back of each tread to allow room for a riser—typically 6 to 8 inches, depending on the material you use to build the steps.

13 DIG OUT THE REMAINING STEPS. Continue to excavate the other steps the same way, measuring up the riser height and using your layout lines as guides. Level the ground roughly from front to back and side to side on each tread, using a level on a straight 2×4.

Building timber-and-paver steps

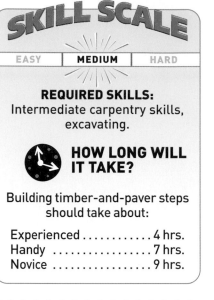
Tread sizes for timber steps

SINGLE TREAD	DOUBLE TREAD
14"–16"	28"–32"

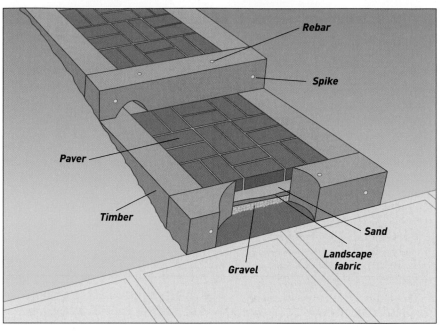

THESE STEPS ARE BUILT WITH 5½-INCH RISERS—the actual size of a 6×6 timber. A tread depth of 29½ inches accommodates three 8-inch-long pavers plus the thickness of a riser, so there's no need to cut pavers. The 2-inch-thick pavers sit flush with the top of the timber frames, resting on a gravel-and-sand bed. Each frame consists of a front piece the width of the step, two side pieces the depth of the tread, and a back piece cut to fit between the sides. The frames are assembled with spikes and anchored into the ground with No. 4 (½-inch) rebar.

The rise of a timber step is a Goldilocks story: Steps made from 4×4s are too low, steps made from 8×8s are too high, but steps made from 6×6s are just right. Given that, few choices are available for the width of the treads. Those shown in the chart are the best choices.

When in doubt, choose a double-length tread. (The length is measured from the riser to the front edge of the stair.) Double treads are easy to climb because you take a step between risers. Depending on the length of the steps, however, double treads may not be possible. If your steps have a run of 48 inches, for example, no combination of 32-inch steps will work. Instead use a single tread: three 16-inch treads fit perfectly.

You can adjust the size of the tread a little. The narrowest it can be is 5½ inches (the true width of a 6×6) plus the length of a paver. If you want to make it wider, make it wider by the full size—width or length—of the paver you're using. If necessary you can make the stairs a bit

longer or shorter. Exactly where you start or stop on a hill is usually a matter of choice.

Building timber-and-paver steps doesn't require specialized skills, but it is labor intensive.

Make the frames of .40 pressure-treated 6×6s, nailing the corners together with 12-inch spikes. Anchor the timbers to the ground with 24-inch lengths of No. 4 (½-inch) rebar. The pavers are standard installation: Lay down landscape fabric, add and compact gravel, and prepare the sand base so the pavers are flush with the top of the timbers.

Adapt timber steps to their surroundings by choosing pavers of different colors. Steps don't just have to be red.

1 **LAY OUT STEPS.** Design the steps with a riser height of 5½ inches and with a tread length from the chart on page 164. Lay out each step with stakes or batterboards and mason's line. Excavate rough steps in the hill. Dig the first tread 6 inches longer than the actual tread measurement (front to back). Dig the others the length of the tread.

2 **BUILD THE FRAMES.** Assemble a 6×6 timber frame for each step, making it 5½ inches longer than the actual tread size. To make sure the frame is the right size, build a corner of the frame and square it with a framing square. Dry-lay your paver pattern against it and position the remaining parts of the frame about 1⁄16 inch from the pavers.

3 **DRILL HOLES AND FINISH ASSEMBLY.** Drill holes slightly narrower and shorter than 12-inch spikes, then spike the corners together. Drill ½-inch holes through the top and out the bottom of the timbers for No. 4 (½-inch) rebar that you'll drive in later.

4 **POSITION THE FRAMES.** Put the first frame in place at the bottom of the stairs. Level it from side to side. Slope it down toward the front by ¼ inch per foot. Test the slope with a 2-foot level that has a ½-inch spacer under one end. The slope is correct when the bubble is centered.

5 **STAKE THE FRAME TO THE GROUND.** Drive 24-inch lengths of No. 4 rebar through the timbers and into the ground. Mark the positions of the rebar in chalk on the back of the timbers so you don't hit the rebar with spikes when nailing in the next frame.

6 **INSTALL THE SECOND STEP.** Set the front timber of the next step on the back of the first. Fasten them together by drilling pilot holes and then driving a pair of 12-inch spikes through the front of the tread. Anchor the back piece with rebar.

Building timber-and-paver steps *(continued)*

PATIOS

7 **INSTALL THE REST OF THE STEPS.** Put the steps in place one at a time. Check that each is level from side to side. Slope each step for drainage.

8 **FILL WITH GRAVEL AND SAND.** Tamp the soil with a hand tamper to compact any loose soil. Put a layer of landscape fabric on the soil, shovel a 1½-inch layer of gravel into the frames, and tamp it. Add about 2 inches of sand over the fabric.

9 **SMOOTH OUT THE SAND.** Build a screed by nailing a 1×4 to a 2×4 so the 1×4 extends below the 2×4 by the thickness of a paver. Screed the sand level.

10 **LAY THE PAVERS.** Lay the pavers in the desired pattern. Bed them in the sand with a rubber mallet.

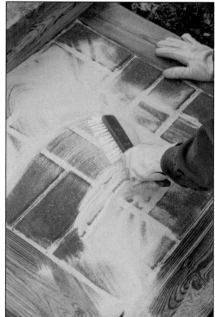

11 **FILL THE JOINTS WITH SAND.** Sweep mason's sand onto the pavers. Spray the steps with water to wash sand into the joints and to compact it. Sweep away the excess sand when it is dry and repeat the process, if necessary.

Designer Tip

SOLID TIMBER STEPS
Full timbers make excellent steps that are easy to install. Excavate rough steps in the ground and add a 4-inch base of tamped gravel. Lay the timbers and fasten them together with spikes. Anchor the timbers by driving 24-inch lengths of No. 4 (½-inch) rebar through predrilled holes into the ground.

Pouring concrete steps

NOT WIDE ENOUGH

Steps are usually designed to be wide
enough for two people to walk
comfortably side-by-side. If your
steps are too narrow you can fix them
while you're installing the forms.
Once the concrete is poured,
however, you'll be walking single file.
Review the details before you do the
installation. Doing the job once
correctly is far more satisfying than
doing it twice to fix a mistake.

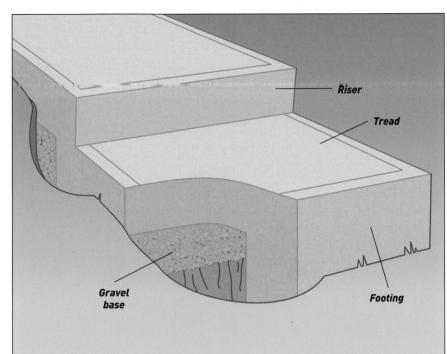

**THE FORMS BUILT TO POUR STEPS ARE SIMILAR TO THE STRINGERS MADE FOR
WOODEN STEPS.** Wet concrete is heavy, and bracing the forms, as shown, is essential.
Remove the forms while the concrete is still wet to trowel and broom the surface.

The steps shown here are garden
steps designed to go up a
hillside but not to be attached to
any structures. Steps attached to
structures require footings and sidewalls.
Local codes govern installation. Attached
steps are best left to the pros.

Garden steps are typically 48 inches
wide so they can accommodate two
people walking side by side.

Steps are made of treads and risers.
The tread is what you walk on; the riser is
the wall at the back of the step. The total
height of the stairs is the rise; the length,
or run, is measured horizontally rather
than along the ground.

For steps with a rise of fewer than 30
inches, a combination of an 11-inch
tread and a 7½-inch riser is the most
comfortable to climb. Steps with a rise of
more than 30 inches are more work to
climb. The ideal riser height is 6 inches;

the ideal tread is 12 inches. For more on
treads and risers, see pages 160–161.

The forms needed for concrete steps
are similar to the risers made for wood
steps. They're laid out the same way, then
the lines are adjusted so the tread slopes
forward and the riser slopes backward.
This creates a tread that won't puddle in
the rain, while moving the riser back to
prevent stubbing your toes.

The total volume of a stairway is
huge, but the concrete is only 4 inches
thick. Masons partially fill the form with
stones to save time, labor, and concrete.

As you'll discover, the forms get in the
way of troweling the concrete. Trowel the
surface as best you can, wait a while, then
remove the forms when the concrete
can support its own weight. The rest
of the finishing, including a nonskid
broomed surface, takes place after the
forms are removed.

Pouring concrete steps *(continued)*

1 **SET UP STAKES AND LINE.** Lay out the sides of the stairs with mason's line and 2×2 stakes set in the ground about 6 inches past the top and bottom of the slope. Position the mason's line so that it runs level from the base of the top stakes to the upper end of the bottom stakes.

2 **LAY OUT THE LENGTH OF THE STAIRS.** Put landscape spikes in the ground to mark the top and bottom of one side of the stairs. Transfer the mark to the layout lines with a plumb bob and mark them with tape. Drive stakes and stretch lines marking the front and back of the stairs, squaring them with a framing square.

3 **MEASURE THE RISE.** Measure the distance from the tape to the ground in inches. The distance is the total rise of the stairway.

4 **MEASURE THE RUN.** Have a helper stand at the top of the hill holding one end of a tape measure while you stand at the bottom holding the other end. Measure between the pieces of tape (in inches) to figure the total run of the stairs.

5 **BUILD A GRAVEL BED.** Sprinkle sand on the ground about 6 inches outside the layout lines. Remove the grass and at least 6 inches of soil, letting the bottom of the excavation follow the slope of the ground. Fill the excavation with gravel in 2-inch layers, compacting between layers, until the gravel is at grade level.

6 **CALCULATE THE SIZE OF THE RISERS.** Divide the total rise by 7½ inches (the ideal riser height). Round up to get the number of risers. Then divide the total rise by the number of risers to get the height of each riser. Mark the height on the narrow arm of a framing square using a stair gauge. (Divide by 6 if the total rise is more than 30 inches.)

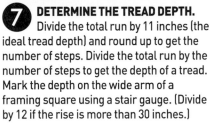

7 **DETERMINE THE TREAD DEPTH.** Divide the total run by 11 inches (the ideal tread depth) and round up to get the number of steps. Divide the total run by the number of steps to get the depth of a tread. Mark the depth on the wide arm of a framing square using a stair gauge. (Divide by 12 if the rise is more than 30 inches.)

8 **LAY OUT THE BOTTOM OF EACH FORM.** You will need two stepped forms; lay out and cut one as directed here, then repeat to build the other. Start by putting the square against the edge of a 2×12, as shown, and draw a line marking the bottom of the form. Extend the line across the board as seen in Step 9.

9 **LAY OUT THE FIRST STEP.** Slide the square along the edge of the form until the gauge on the wide arm meets the line you drew. Trace along the wide arm to lay out the tread. Trace along the narrow arm to lay out the riser.

10 **LAY OUT THE NEXT STEP.** Move the square farther up the form. Slide the framing square until the gauge on the wide arm meets the line marking the riser of the first step. Trace along the square, outlining the rise and the run. Repeat the process for each step.

11 **LAY OUT THE TOP OF THE FORM.** Once you've drawn the line for the last riser, extend it across the form to mark the top end of the form.

12 **DRAW IN THE SLOPE.** The back of the treads should be ¼ inch higher than the front so water will run off. Measure up this amount at the back of each tread and draw a new tread. Slope the riser in 1 inch at the bottom for extra foot room.

Pouring concrete steps (continued)

13 **CUT OUT THE TOP AND BOTTOM OF THE FORM.** Set your circular saw to cut through the form. Cut along the layout line that marks the top of the form. Move to the other end of the form and cut along the line marking the bottom of the form.

14 **CUT OUT THE RISERS.** Cut along the layout lines that mark the risers. Stop when the blade reaches the layout line for the tread. Repeat to cut out the treads, stopping when the saw cut reaches the layout line marking the riser.

15 **FINISH THE CUTS BY HAND.** Because of the shape of the blade, the saw will leave an uncut section of wood on the back of the form. Finish the cut with a handsaw.

16 **CUT RISER FORMS.** The forms need boards nailed across the front of the risers to hold back the wet concrete. Cut 2×8s to the length and height of the risers. Bevel an edge so the boards don't cover the step below.

17 **INSTALL THE SIDES.** Put the side forms in place. Nail a riser across the front and back of the forms. Square the assembly with a framing square and level the forms side to side.

18 **INSTALL THE RISERS.** Stake the sides every 4 feet on center and nail the stakes to them with duplex nails, which remove easily. Nail the risers in place starting at the top so you won't stand on risers you just installed. Coat the forms with a form-release agent or vegetable oil so they will be easy to remove from the dried concrete.

FILLING THE FORMS

1 **PUT STONE IN THE FORMS.** Save on the concrete you'll need by partially filling the forms with 1- to 2-inch stones. Keep the stones at least 4 inches from the sides and tops of the forms. Wet the stones just before putting in the concrete to keep them from sucking water from the concrete.

2 **FILL THE BOTTOM STEP WITH CONCRETE.** Mix enough concrete to fill the entire form, following the directions on the bag. Fill the bottom step first, overfilling it slightly. Work a shovel up and down to remove trapped air.

3 **TROWEL THE SURFACE SMOOTH.** Strike the concrete level with the top of the step with a trowel. Fill the steps, one at a time, the way you filled the first.

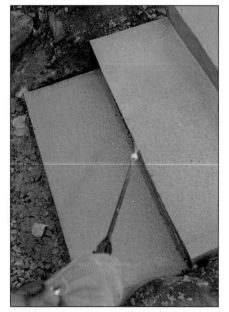

4 **TROWEL THE CONCRETE.** After about one hour, remove the front riser. If the concrete sags, put the riser back, and test again later. When the concrete can support its own weight, remove the forms entirely, and smooth the concrete with a mason's trowel until water forms on the surface.

5 **BROOM THE SURFACE.** Wait until the sheen is gone from the surface. Round over all edges of each step with an edger. Pull a damp stiff-bristled broom across the treads perpendicular to traffic to give them a non-skid surface.

6 **APPLY CURING COMPOUND.** Pour a curing compound into a garden sprayer and spray it onto the steps while the concrete is still wet. The compound keeps moisture in the concrete so that it won't crack as it hardens. Allow to cure 5 days in warm weather and 7 days in cold weather before walking on the steps.

Laying mortared brick or stone steps

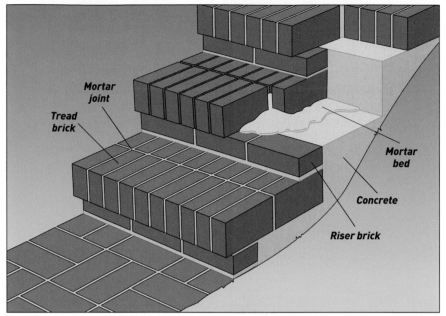

Mortared brick or stone steps are laid on concrete. Construct concrete steps as shown on pages 167–171. For bricks try to plan for a riser height of 6½ inches and a tread depth of about 12½ inches. Don't finish the concrete; the mortar will adhere better to a rough surface.

Excavate 6 inches around the steps to install forms, setting them ½ inch above the concrete for bricks and 1 inch above for stones. Apply a bed of mortar, screed it, and lay the bricks or stones. Use face bricks rather than paver bricks, which are too smooth for stairs. Use bricks rated SW or SX in climates that have severe weather conditions; MW or MX bricks are acceptable in moderate climates where there is no freezing. If you apply stone, choose bluestone or slate.

Labels on illustration: Mortar joint · Tread brick · Mortar bed · Concrete · Riser brick

CONCRETE IS THE STEP FOUNDATION AND PREVENTS THE MORTAR FROM CRACKING DUE TO GROUND SHIFTS OR FREEZING AND THAWING. Mortar holds bricks or stones to the concrete and fills the spaces between them. A rowlock pattern—bricks placed on edge—is strong, durable, and the most common way to lay bricks on steps. If using stones, choose large, flat stones at least 1 inch thick. Lay a ½-inch-thick mortar bed for bricks, a 1-inch-thick bed for stones. Bricks or stones on treads can overlap risers by 1 to 2 inches as long as the overlap is equal on each step.

SKILL SCALE

EASY | **MEDIUM** | HARD

REQUIRED SKILLS:
Intermediate masonry skills.

HOW LONG WILL IT TAKE?

Building three mortared brick or stone steps should take about:

Experienced . . . . 8 hrs.
Handy . . . . 12 hrs.
Novice . . . . 15 hrs.

STUFF YOU'LL NEED

✔ **MATERIALS:**
1¼-inch screws, duplex nails, 2×4, plywood, Type M mortar, bricks, flat stones, cement slurry

✔ **TOOLS:**
Hammer, mixing tub, mason's trowel, screed, level, rubber mallet, 3-pound sledgehammer, brick chisel, mortar bag, paintbrush, jointer, work gloves, safety glasses, burlap rag, carpenter's pencil

LAYING MORTARED BRICK STEPS

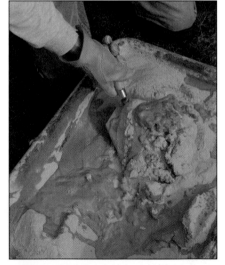

1 BUILD FORMS FOR THE MORTAR. Put form boards against the sides of the concrete steps with the tops of the forms ½ inch—the thickness of the mortar bed—above the steps. Hold the boards in place with 2×4 stakes driven into the ground. Attach the stakes to the forms with 1¼ inch screws or duplex nails.

2 MIX MORTAR. Pour a bag of premixed Type M mortar into a mixing tub. Make a small well in the middle of the mix and gradually add water, stirring with a trowel. The instructions on the bag will indicate how much water to add. When the mortar clings to a trowel set on edge, it is the right consistency.

3 **APPLY BRICKS TO THE FIRST RISER.** Lay the mortar and bricks for one riser and tread at a time. Spread about ½ inch of mortar along the face of the first riser. Then spread the same amount of mortar on the bottom and ends of individual bricks and put them against the riser.

4 **APPLY MORTAR TO THE FIRST TREAD.** Spread ½ inch of mortar on the first tread. Pull a screed across the forms to level the mortar. Trowel mortar on the top of the riser bricks you just laid, up to the height of the tread.

5 **LAY BRICKS ACROSS THE FIRST TREAD.** Space them ⅜ inch to ½ inch apart with plywood spacers, positioning them as shown. Tap the bricks in place with a rubber mallet to level them with each other and to embed them in the mortar.

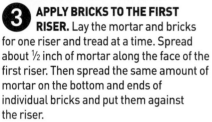

6 **BUILD MORE STEPS AND MORTAR BETWEEN THE BRICKS.** Put a 2×4 across the tread to check for high and low spots. To fix a low spot, add mortar. For a high spot, tap the brick with the rubber mallet. Continue to lay bricks this way until the steps are complete, then remove the form boards and spacers. Using a mortar bag, fill the joints between bricks with mortar.

7 **TOOL THE JOINTS.** Smooth and compress the joints with a convex jointer, working from back to front. Before the mortar dries, wipe any excess mortar from the bricks with a dry burlap rag. Cover with a sheet of plastic and let the mortar harden for three to four days. Wait one week before using the steps.

Designer Tip

BRICK PATTERNS
You can create variety on your steps by laying the bricks in different patterns. Do a dry run first to make sure the bricks align properly.

Laying mortared brick or stone steps (continued)

LAYING MORTARED STONE STEPS

1 **FIT THE STONES.** Install forms that extend one inch above the mortar bed and test-fit the stones on both treads and risers. Mark where stones need to be cut using a carpenter's pencil. Stones on the treads can overhang those on the risers by 1 to 2 inches. Number the stones so you can reposition them correctly.

2 **CUT THE STONES.** Score cut lines along the pencil marks by striking them with a brick chisel and a 3-pound sledgehammer. Then prop the scored section over a scrap piece of wood or pipe and break it off with a sharp blow from the sledgehammer. (For more on cutting stone, see page 30.)

3 **APPLY MORTAR.** Mix Type M mortar in a tub and spread about 1 inch on the first riser and tread. Draw a screed across the forms to level the mortar. Brush the bottom of each stone with a cream-textured slurry made of portland cement and water to help the stones stick to the mortar.

4 **LAY THE FIRST STEP.** Put the first stones against the riser. Tap them gently with a rubber mallet to help embed them evenly with each other in the mortar. Place stones on the tread the same way.

5 **APPLY MORTAR BETWEEN THE STONES.** Working one riser and tread at a time, continue setting stones as in Step 4 until the steps are laid. Remove the form boards, then use a trowel to pack the joints between the stones with mortar.

6 **TOOL THE JOINTS.** Smooth and compress the joints with a concave jointer. Wipe off excess mortar with a damp rag. Cover with a sheet of plastic and let dry for three to four days. Keep foot traffic off the steps for one week.

Building a wheelchair ramp

REQUIRED SKILLS:
Layout, excavation, basic carpentry, and concrete work.

 HOW LONG WILL IT TAKE?

Building a ramp 20 feet long and 20 inches high should take about:

Experienced . . . . 6 days
Handy . . . . 10 days
Novice . . . . 12 days

STUFF YOU'LL NEED

✔ MATERIALS:

¾-inch gravel, landscape fabric, fiber tube forms, premixed concrete, pressure-treated 1×s, 2×s, 4×4s, and ⁵⁄₄×6 decking, galvanized 10d (3-inch) nails, 8d (2½-inch) nails or No. 8 2-inch deck screws, seismic anchors/hurricane ties, ⅜×7-inch hex-head bolts, washers and nuts, joist hangers, 1½-inch handrail, handrail brackets

✔ TOOLS:

Tape measure, mason's line, line level, plumb bob, 3-pound sledgehammer, mattock, spade or shovel, garden rake, posthole digger, wheelbarrow, circular saw, handsaw, framing square, combination square, 4-foot level, ⅜-inch electric drill and bits, speed square, hammer, ratchet and socket wrenches, safety glasses, work gloves, dust mask, mason's hoe, darby, wood float, concrete broom, concrete edger

Ramps, usually constructed for wheelchairs, are also ideal for strollers, and they can add resale value to your home. The Americans with Disabilities Act sets strict standards for ramps. The slope, for example, must be no more than 1 inch per foot. Ramps, therefore, tend to be long. You'll need a ramp at least 20 feet long to reach a deck 20 inches high. Construct the ramp with pressure-treated lumber, using posts rated for ground contact. Before you start building be sure to check your local codes for requirements.

This 43-inch-wide wheelchair ramp provides access from ground level to a deck 20 inches high. A level 5×5-foot landing at the top accommodates turning. Pairs of pressure-treated 4×4 posts set in concrete every 5 feet on center hold 2×6 crosspieces that support a framework of 2×6 joists. The posts are cut tall enough to hold 2×4 side and 2×6 cap rails as well as handrails 36 inches above the decking.

INSTALLING POSTS

Meeting design requirements

The following requirements are determined by the Americans with Disabilities Act (ADA). Design your ramp accordingly.

■ **Rise:** A maximum of 1 inch rise for every 12 inches of run. A rise of 1 inch for every 20 inches is ideal.
■ **Width:** A minimum clearance of 36 inches between handrails or curbs.
■ **Landings:** A minimum level area of 60×60 inches for every 30 inches of rise and for every change of direction.
■ **Surfaces:** Slip-resistant and flush with adjacent surfaces at top and bottom.
■ **Handrails:** Continuous, 1¼ to 1½ inches in diameter, round or oval, 34 to 38 inches high on both sides, and extending 12 inches beyond end points.

1 **DETERMINE THE LENGTH.**
Measure up from the ground to determine how many inches the ramp must rise. For every inch of rise, you'll need at least a foot of run. A 20-inch-high deck, for example, requires a 20-foot-long ramp. A slope of 1:20 would require a ramp 33⅓ feet long.

Building a wheelchair ramp

INSTALLING POSTS *(continued)*

Ramp specs

- **Width:** 43 inches.
- **Length:** Measure up from the ground to the porch or deck to find how many inches the ramp must rise. A 1:20-inch slope requires 20 inches of run for every inch of height.
- **Posts:** 4×4s, spaced 5 feet on center along the length of the ramp and 39½ inches across the width.
- **Crosspieces:** Two 2×6s bolted to opposite sides of the posts with tops beveled to follow the slope of the walk.
- **Joists:** Four 2×6 joists, running the length of the ramp.
- **Decking:** ⁵⁄₄ deck boards.

2 **LAY OUT THE LANDING.** To accommodate turning at the top of the ramp, lay out a 5-foot-square landing with batterboards and mason's lines. Level each line and use the 3-4-5 triangle to square the lines with the house. Slide the lines along the batterboards until the distance between two points 3 feet and 4 feet from the corner is 5 feet. (See page 38.)

3 **LAY OUT THE OUTSIDE EDGES OF THE RAMP** with batterboards and mason's lines. Level the lines and square them using the 3-4-5 triangle. Remove the sod from the site and dig out 2 to 3 inches of soil. Dig a few inches deeper at the bottom of the ramp so you can build as close to ground level as possible.

4 **LAY OUT THE POSTS.** Plant posts against the house, porch, or deck that the ramp will lead to, at the corners of the landing, and every 5 feet on center along the length of the ramp. Lay out the posts with mason's lines and masking tape. Transfer the taped marks to the ground with a plumb bob and powdered chalk.

5 **DIG FOR FOOTINGS.** Mark the position of the mason's lines on the batterboards and untie them. Dig holes for posts at least 6 inches below the frost line, tapering them from 12 inches at the top to 18 inches at the bottom. Reattach the lines and move the tape 1¾ inches so it marks the location of the outside face of the posts.

6 **POUR FOOTINGS.** Cut fiber tube forms 6 inches shorter than the holes are deep. Nail 2×4s to opposite sides of the forms and suspend the forms in the holes so they sit about 8 inches from the bottom. Put posts in the holes, and plumb and brace them. Fill the tubes with bagged concrete, mixed according to the directions on the bag. Remove the forms after 48 hours and fill in the holes.

PATIOS

BUILDING A FRAME AND ADDING DECKING

1 **BUILD THE LANDING.** Code requires a landing at the top of the ramp so wheelchair users can get through doors easily. Run crosspieces from post to post across the ramp and bolt them to the posts. Install joists on top. Position the landing so the decking will be flush with the door threshold.

2 **LAY OUT THE CROSSPIECES AND JOISTS.** Snap a chalk line from the top of the crosspiece at the landing to the ground at the bottom of the ramp to show where the crosspieces and joists will meet each post. Snap a chalk line 5½ inches higher to show the top of the joists.

3 **LAY OUT THE BEVEL OF THE CROSSPIECES.** The crosspieces are beveled so the joists rest on the entire top surface of the crosspiece. Lay out the bevel with a framing square and plywood. Mark 1 inch along the side of the plywood and 12 inches (or the appropriate slope ratio) along the other side. Connect the points with a straight line and set a bevel gauge to the angle.

4 **CUT THE CROSSPIECES.** Measure across the ramp from outside the post to outside the opposite post. Cut the crosspieces to this length. Set the blade on a tablesaw to match the slope of the bevel gauge, and cut the top edge of each board to the angle.

5 **INSTALL THE CROSSPIECES.** Temporarily clamp the crosspieces along the chalk lines that mark the bottom of the joists. Clamp them to several posts, then check their position by resting a joist on them. Reposition any crosspieces that are too high or too low. Clamp them firmly in place; drill ½-inch-diameter holes through the crosspiece, into the post, and out the other side of the second crosspiece. Bolt them in place with ½-inch bolts, nuts, and washers. Install all the crosspieces.

6 **CUT THE UPPER ENDS OF THE JOISTS.** Rest a joist on the crosspieces and butt it up to the landing. Lay out the angle on the end by tracing along a scrap of wood or the arm of a framing square held against the landing. Cut along the line. Repeat for the other joists.

Building a wheelchair ramp

BUILDING A FRAME AND ADDING DECKING *(continued)*

7 **LAY OUT THE SPLICE ON THE OUTER JOIST.** If the outer joist isn't long enough, you'll have to splice two joists together. Mark the center of the post and transfer the mark to the joist. Make a square cut at the joist to cut it to length.

8 **LAY OUT THE SECOND HALF OF THE SPLICE.** Temporarily put the next joist in place. Trace along the joist you just cut to lay out the angle you need on the mating joist. Nail or screw reinforcement along the seam.

9 **INSTALL INNER JOISTS.** If you need to splice joists, cut the spliced end to extend beyond the crosspiece by at least 8 inches. Position the next joist so it overlaps the crosspiece by an equal amount. Nail the two together. Nail joists to crosspieces with seismic anchors/hurricane ties.

10 **CUT THE ENDS OF THE JOISTS.** Trace along the posts to lay out the end of the outside joists. Temporarily position the inner joist against the post, too, and trace along it to lay out the cut. Cut the joists to length with a circular saw. Attach all the joists to the crosspieces with seismic anchors/hurricane ties.

11 **CUT AND INSTALL AN END JOIST.** Cut a piece to fit across the end of the ramp. Nail or screw it to the ends of the joists.

12 **ATTACH THE DECKING.** Nail or screw the deck boards to the joists with galvanized 8d (2½-inch) nails or No. 8 2-inch deck screws. Butt the boards together; because they're pressure-treated, they will shrink as they dry, leaving about an ⅛-inch gap for drainage.

ADDING RAILINGS

① **SNAP A CHALK LINE TO MARK THE TOP OF THE POSTS.** Measure 40 inches up from the decking and mark the top post. Repeat at the bottom. Snap a chalk line between the marks. Repeat on the other side of the posts and on the other set of posts.

② **CUT THE POSTS.** To cut each post clamp a speed square in place to follow the slope of the chalk line and to support your circular saw with the blade at the cut line. Saw across the face of the post. The cut won't go all the way through, so repeat on the other side of the post.

③ **INSTALL THE RAILS.** Install 2×4 side rails along the inner faces of the posts with galvanized 10d (3-inch) nails. Put one rail at the top, another at the bottom no higher than 4 inches above the decking, and the other two evenly spaced between the top and bottom.

④ **ATTACH THE HANDRAIL.** Cut a piece of 2×4 to fit between the upper two rails on each post. Screw the 2×4s in place, then screw brackets for a 1½-inch handrail to them, positioning the rail 34 to 38 inches above the decking. Screw a handrail to each side of the ramp.

⑤ **ATTACH THE CAP RAILS.** Nail 2×6 cap rails to the tops of the posts with galvanized 10d (3-inch) nails. Set them flush with the inner faces of the posts, and miter the corners. Toenail the mitered corners together with galvanized 8d (2½-inch) nails.

⑥ **POUR A CONCRETE RAMP.** Dig for and install a 4-inch gravel bed, then build forms and pour concrete for a 4-inch-thick ramp that runs from the end of the wooden ramp to ground level. Screed the concrete and give it a broom finish. (For more on concrete, see "Building a Concrete Walk," beginning on page 86.)

REPAIR AND MAINTENANCE

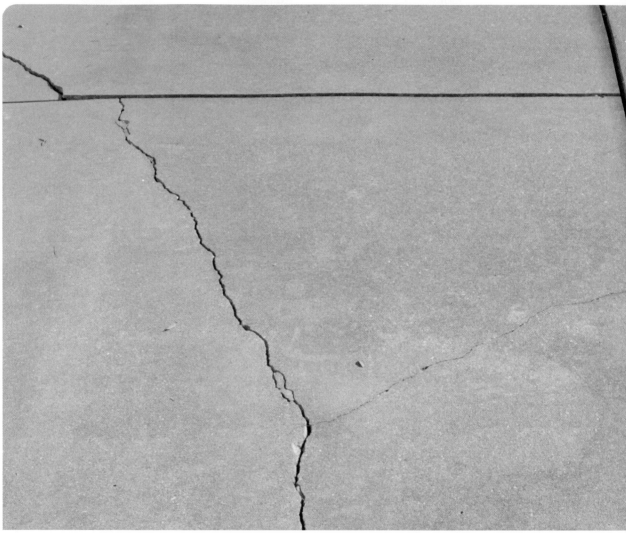

Pavers, bricks, or a concrete slab may seem indestructible as you recall almost every brick you laid or the number of bags of concrete it took to pour a foundation. No matter how permanent the elements of your patio or walkway may appear, however, over time they will begin to deteriorate and show signs of age. You may notice these signs of deterioration:

- The sand filling the joints on a soft-set walkway or patio disappears and has to be replaced.
- Mortar joints crumble on a hard-bed installation and you need to clean them out and reapply fresh mortar.
- Bricks or pavers crack and have to be removed and replaced with new ones.
- Inevitable cracks appear in a concrete slab, or sections of the slab shift and need to be repaired.
- Materials used in soft-set installations shift and need to be releveled or replaced.

- Pressure-treated lumber used in a boardwalk requires replacement.

Fortunately most of the problems caused by age and weather conditions can be repaired. Numerous products make repairing and maintaining your outdoor projects easier.

In this section you'll find information about repairing sand beds, refilling joints, and replacing bricks, stone, tile, and pavers. Also included are instructions for replacing concrete, repairing cracks, and replacing boards in a boardwalk.

Of course the best way to avoid mistakes that can lead to costly repairs is to do the job right the first time. Do what you can to make installation and repair easy for yourself, and remember, you can't control the elements.

REAL-WORLD SITUATIONS

KEEPING UP WITH MOTHER NATURE

Maintenance and repair tasks are easier if you do what needs to be done before conditions deteriorate to a point that an entire installation needs to be replaced. Rather than rip out a patio or walkway, unless you're tired of the old patio, however, it's easier to replace a few chipped or damaged bricks than it is to start from scratch.

■ As long as the foundation or base of the patio or walkway is secure, the surface usually can be repaired. If the base is weak due to drainage problems, heaving from seasonal weather changes, or a pesky tree root, it may require a new installation.

■ Minor cracking in a concrete slab usually doesn't affect its stability; settling occurs naturally. Fill the crack, seal it, and forget about it.

■ Preservatives used in pressure-treated lumber don't penetrate through to the core, making cut ends vulnerable to rot and decay. Coat them with a sealer before installation to lengthen the life of your project.

■ Wear proper clothing and protective gear while you work on repairs. Long-sleeve shirts and gloves are essential when handling concrete or cutting pressure-treated lumber. Also recommended for these tasks are a dust mask, safety glasses, and a hat.

Maintaining walks and patios

Whether you use your walk or patio every day of the year or only during the summer, it's exposed to the elements year-round. Eventually it needs maintenance. Both traffic and weather affect walks and patios. Freezing, thawing, and rain attack the most vulnerable spot—the joints. Watch for small problems with the sand between pavers or the mortar along stones, and you'll avoid larger problems later.

SKILL SCALE

EASY	MEDIUM	HARD

REQUIRED SKILLS:
Basic masonry skills.

HOW LONG WILL IT TAKE?

An average repair on a 4×5-foot area should take about:

Experienced . . . . 30 min.
Handy . . . . 1 hr.
Novice . . . . 2 hrs.

STUFF YOU'LL NEED

✔ **MATERIALS:**
Mortar, mason's sand, grout, thinset, 2×4, bonding agent, concrete, duplex nails, gravel, expansion joint, wire mesh, burlap

✔ **TOOLS:**
Stiff-bristle brush, putty knife, rubber mallet, hose, point punch, cold chisel, brick chisel, plugging chisel, pointing trowel, jointer, 3-pound and 7-pound sledgehammers, mixing tub, mortar bag, carbide scoring tool, straightedge, grout float, metal or wooden float, work gloves, safety glasses, dust mask, knee pads

CLEANING PAVERS

PULL WEEDS OUT OF THE JOINTS by sliding a putty knife along the gaps between the bricks. (If you place landscaping fabric under your walk when building it, you will rarely encounter this problem.)

CLEAN STAINS FROM THE WALK WITH A STIFF-BRISTLE BRUSH and warm, soapy water. For tough stains use diluted (1:9) muriatic acid or a trisodium phosphate (TSP) solution. Don't use acid on stone surfaces—it may stain. A stubborn stain on stone or brick often can be removed by rubbing it with a piece of similar stone or brick.

REPAIRING SAND-BED PAVING

1 REMOVE THE PAVER. Sometimes part of a walk or patio will sink a little, creating a low spot. To correct the problem remove the lowest paver by prying it loose with a cold chisel or screwdriver.

2 ADD AND LEVEL SAND. After you remove all the low bricks, add sand. Level the area to the height of the surrounding bed and screed the sand bed with a notched 2×4 resting the ends of the 2×4 on the nearby bricks or pavers.

3 **REPLACE THE PAVERS.** Tap the pavers back into place with a rubber mallet. Check their position relative to their neighbors with a straight 2×4. If one or more pavers are uneven, add or remove sand beneath them until they are even with the surrounding pavers.

4 **FILL IN WITH SAND.** Sprinkle mason's sand over the restored area. Sweep the sand into the joints with a stiff-bristle brush. Spray the walk with water to settle the sand firmly into the joints. Add more sand and respray, if necessary.

Designer Tip

MAKING NEW BRICK LOOK OLD
When adding new bricks to an older pattern, the color and texture may not match. Soak new bricks in sandy or muddy water to give them the color of older bricks. Rubbing sand against the bricks gives the surface a worn look and prevents the coloring from rubbing away easily. Also try rubbing a few of the newer bricks against one another to age them.

REPAIRING MORTAR JOINTS

SAFETY ALERT

When chipping mortar, wear work gloves and safety glasses.

1 **CHISEL OUT THE OLD MORTAR.** Remove damaged mortar from around bricks with a 3-pound sledgehammer and a cold chisel. Work carefully, removing only as much mortar as necessary.

2 **CLEAN THE SURFACE.** After you chisel away the mortar, sweep away loose particles with a stiff-bristle brush or whisk.

3 **MIX MORTAR.** In a mixing tub mix one part portland cement and three parts mason's sand. Add water, blending the materials together until the mortar is workable yet stiff. For small jobs use premixed mortar.

REPAIR AND MAINTENANCE

Maintaining walks and patios

REPAIRING MORTAR JOINTS (continued)

FILL WITH MORTAR. Fill the joints with a mortar bag, also known as a blow bag. Squeeze the bag gently and evenly so you don't use too much mortar; excess mortar is hard to clean up.

5 TOOL THE JOINTS. Strike the joints with a jointer that matches the profile of the original joint. Start the strike on an old joint and follow through into the new mortar so the new joint looks like the old ones.

Cleaning concrete

Commercial cleaning agents, when used with rented power washers, are good for general cleaning. Some stains, such as the chalky, salty residue after a rainfall, can be brushed off with a stiff-bristle brush. For oil and grease stains, scrub the stain with mineral spirits, sprinkle it with kitty litter or sand, then sweep it up. Stains that have penetrated can be dissolved with commercial cleaners. Remove rust stains with bleach and a stiff-bristle scrub brush.

REPLACING A BRICK, STONE, OR TILE

SAFETY ● ALERT

Wear safety glasses when breaking up pavers, mortar, or concrete.

1 REMOVE THE MORTAR OR GROUT. Replacing brick, stone, and tile are much the same. Chisel out the mortar around brick or stone with a plugging chisel. Remove the grout around tile with a grout saw.

2 BREAK UP THE PAVER. Remove a damaged brick or stone by breaking it into smaller pieces with a hammer and cold chisel. Score a tile repeatedly on the diagonals with a carbide scoring tool and straightedge until the line is $1/16$ inch deep. Strike in the middle with a point punch and hammer. Break up the rest of it with a cold chisel.

3 REMOVE THE MORTAR. Chip away the mortar or thinset with a brick chisel. The resulting surface doesn't need to be perfect; remove enough to make room for a new bed of mortar or thinset.

4 **REPLACE THE MORTAR OR THINSET.** Apply a ½-inch layer of mortar for use under brick or stone. Apply thinset under tile, combing it out with a trowel that has notches the same size as the tile's thickness.

4 **SET THE PAVER.** Put the brick, stone, or tile in place. Use a straightedge to make sure it is the same height as the surrounding pavers. Tap with a rubber mallet to set it deeper; add mortar or thinset, if necessary, to raise it.

6 **APPLY MORTAR OR GROUT.** Fill in around bricks or stone with mortar and tool it to match the surrounding mortar. When replacing a tile remove the thinset around the tile while it is still wet. Once the thinset under the tile has dried, apply grout with a grout float. After 15 minutes clean the tile with a scrub pad and water to remove excess grout.

REPAIRING SMALL CRACKS IN CONCRETE

Wear gloves and safety glasses when chiseling concrete and when working with acids.

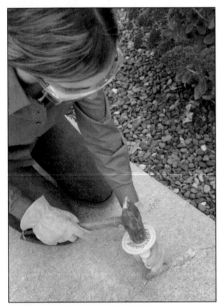

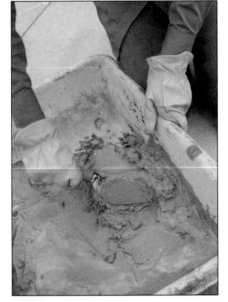

1 **PREPARE THE CRACKS.** Fill cracks less than ⅛ inch wide with latex or epoxy patching compound, following the manufacturer's instructions. Larger cracks need to be undercut with a cold chisel angled slightly outward. Rap it with a 3-pound sledgehammer, widening the crack at the bottom.

2 **APPLY MORTAR.** Sweep the crack clean with a stiff-bristle brush, dampen it, then brush the surface with a concrete bonding agent. Wait 15 minutes before adding mortar to the crack. Prepare mortar by mixing one part portland cement and three parts mason's sand. Add enough water to make a thick paste. For small jobs use premixed mortar.

3 **SMOOTH THE SURFACE.** Trowel on the mortar and smooth the surface with either a metal or wooden float.

Maintaining walks and patios *(continued)*

REPLACING CONCRETE

1 **REMOVE THE CONCRETE.** Break up the damaged section of concrete with a 7-pound sledgehammer. If the area is more than a few square feet, you may want to rent a jackhammer. Break up the concrete into small pieces.

2 **INSTALL FORMS.** Replace the existing gravel and tamp the surface. Install form boards against the existing concrete, holding it in place with 2×4 stakes. Nail the forms to the stakes with duplex nails.

3 **INSTALL REINFORCING MESH.** Place wire mesh on wire supports in the repair area at about the midpoint of the concrete's depth. If the concrete abuts a solid structure, such as a house foundation, place an expansion joint along the edge.

REPAIR AND MAINTENANCE

CURING COMPOUNDS
Curing is the process by which concrete hardens. During this process you must take steps to make sure the concrete does not lose moisture too quickly. Curing products are available at home centers to ensure smooth, even curing of concrete walks and patios. Wax- and resin-based compounds are the most popular. Apply the curing compound with a paintbrush or roller while the concrete is still damp. For larger areas, use a sprayer. Apply a second coat, brushing or spraying perpendicular to the first coat.

4 **POUR THE CONCRETE.** Empty bagged premixed concrete into a wheelbarrow, add water, and mix until the consistency is firm yet workable. Put a bonding agent on the broken edges of the concrete and pour concrete into the damaged area.

5 **SCREED, FINISH, AND CURE.** Screed the surface of the repaired area with a 2×4 so it is smooth and level with surrounding concrete. Float and finish the surface to match the old concrete. Cover the repaired area with a sheet of plastic and allow the concrete to cure for at least one day.

Maintaining boardwalks and ramps

Build a boardwalk or wheelchair ramp well, and it will provide years of service. But don't expect it to be maintenance free. Rain, wind, snow, and sun eventually exact their toll.

Inspect your structure once or twice a year and make repairs as soon as damage is evident. The old saying holds true: An ounce of prevention applies here too.

SKILL SCALE

EASY	MEDIUM	HARD

REQUIRED SKILLS:
Basic carpentry skills.

HOW LONG WILL IT TAKE?

General maintenance of a boardwalk or ramp should take about:

Experienced . . . . 1 hr.
Handy . . . . 2 hrs.
Novice . . . . 3 hrs.

STUFF YOU'LL NEED

✔ MATERIALS:
Brightener, finish, pressure-treated lumber, baking soda, wood putty, premixed concrete, galvanized 10d (3-inch) nails, hex-head bolts, J-bolt, post anchor

✔ TOOLS:
Broom, putty knife, pressure sprayer, scrub brush, bucket, awl, paintbrush, keyhole saw, handsaw, circular saw, hammer, screw jack, level, ⅜-inch drill and bits, wood chisel, trowel, plumb bob, ratchet and socket wrenches, safety glasses, rubber gloves, work gloves, dust mask

CLEANING SURFACES

SWEEP SURFACES REGULARLY, paying particular attention to the decking, stairs, corners, and out-of-the-way spots. To remove dirt and stains, scrub the deck with a solution of mild household detergent and water.

REMOVE DEBRIS FROM BETWEEN BOARDS WITH A PUTTY KNIFE. Debris caught between boards allows water to pool, causing wood to rot.

BRIGHTEN WEATHERED WOOD by applying a commercial deck brightener with a pressure sprayer. Spray, wait 10 minutes, scrub the deck with a stiff-bristle brush, then rinse with cold water. Let the deck dry thoroughly before applying a finish.

APPLY A FINISH either by spray or brush. Use a paintbrush to eliminate drips and to apply the finish in cracks and hard-to-reach areas.

REPLACING DECKING

Rotted, cracked, or insect-damaged decking boards spoil the look of your boardwalk or ramp and can be dangerous. If the damage is limited to a small area, replace a section of the decking rather than an entire board to save time and money without compromising the look or sturdiness of your deck. If the damage is merely cosmetic, you sometimes can remove the deck plank, flip it over, and nail it back in place.

Sawdust and particles from pressure-treated lumber are toxic. Wear a dust mask, gloves, safety glasses, and a long-sleeve shirt when working with the material.

1 LOCATE THE JOISTS ON EACH SIDE OF THE DAMAGED AREA. (Nailheads in the decking are a good indication of where these joists are located.) Drill a starter hole, then use a keyhole saw to cut the board flush with the edges of the joists.

2 TO SUPPORT THE NEW SECTION, fasten a 2×4 cleat to each exposed joist with galvanized 10d (3-inch) nails. Position the cleat flush with the top of the joist.

3 SCRUB THE BOARD with a solution of 1 cup of baking soda and 1 gallon of warm water to give it the same weathered look as the surrounding decking.

4 CUT THE REPLACEMENT BOARD TO FIT, trim it flush with the rest of the decking.

5 ALIGN THE DECKING, then nail the new piece to the cleats with galvanized 10d (3-inch) nails.

Index

Special thanks to the Interlocking Concrete Pavement Institute, 1444 I Street NW, Suite 700, Washington, D.C. 20005-2210, www.icpi.org, for their input on paver patio construction.

INDEX